Robert Hendry

RAILS IN THE

ISLE OF MAN

A Colour Celebration

**One of the most unusual aspects of the
Isle of Man Railway Company was its
diversity. As well as steam trains, it
operated buses, lorries, an amusement
resort, motor boats and even ran its own
football competition, complete with
an imposing cup.**

This book
is respectfully dedicated to the
memory of my father
Dr Robert Preston Hendry

Copyright 1993 Robert Hendry

Published by
Midland Publishing Limited
24 The Hollow, Earl Shilton
Leicester, LE9 7NA
England

ISBN 1-85780-009-5

Printed in England by
The Nuffield Press Limited
Cowley, Oxford
OX4 2PH

Designed by
Midland Publishing
and Stephen Thompson Associates.

Typeset
in 8 on 10 and 9 on 11pt Garamond
and Gill Sans.

Robert Hendry

RAILS IN THE

ISLE OF MAN

A Colour Celebration

Midland Publishing
Limited

The Isle of Man Tramways
& Electric Power Company developed a
'rustic' architectural style all its own.
This 1961 scene shows the station
building at Laxey, with its corrugated iron
roofing and wooden buildings liberally
decorated with half round branches.
It is one of the most notable survivors of
these early structures.

CONTENTS

Front cover:
No 11 *Maitland* leaves Douglas in dramatic style, with the re-opening special on Saturday, 3rd June 1967.

Although badly burnt in September 1990, MER car No 22 was rebuilt and is seen climbing out of Laxey in May 1992.

The preserved horse tramway double decker car No 14 makes a rare appearance in service, in May 1984.

Title page:
No 10 *G H Wood* makes a vigorous start from the Port Erin platform at Douglas station on 19th August 1965, as No 5 *Mona* and No 11 *Maitland* simmer on the shed approach. In its heyday, the bustle and constant activity at Douglas had more in common with a big city terminal than the usual tranquillity of the narrow gauge.

Back cover:
Flanked by stationary MER and SMR cars, IMR locomotive No 4 *Loch* runs past Laxey station, during the special centenary steam event on the Manx Electric Railway, 5th December 1991.
Chris Milner

PREFACE

It must be rare for an author to claim that his first contact with the subject of his book was when he was in his pram. My father even filmed the event, but not alas in colour, so it is not in this book! I grew up knowing many of the people running the railways of the Isle of Man, and a chance comment to my mother, when I was researching for our book on the Manx Northern, revealed that John Cameron, who had been manager of the Manx Northern Railway from 1882 to 1898, had been a friend of her father's. Her father spent much of his childhood in Peel, and as a child, had been present at the opening of the Peel line in 1873. I already knew that Eddie Barnes, chief engineer, and later manager of the Manx Electric Railway was distantly related by marriage, and that my mother and Mr Barnes' daughter regularly stayed at each other's homes, the Barnes house being the MER Engineer's residence.

My father's earliest recollections of the steam railway were in 1917, when his grandfather was on the staff of the Knockaloe Alien Internment Camp near Peel. Grandad used to have leave once a month, and come home by train. My father was very fond of him, but was never sorry if the train was a few minutes late, as a Port Erin train was

due in about the same time, and a late arrival of Grandad's train, meant he saw two trains instead of one!

From the start of the 1950's he filmed the railways of the Isle of Man extensively, and in due course, I 'cut my teeth' using grandfather's Rolleiflex camera. Apart from Ian Macnab's superb history of the Isle of Man Railway, there was little then in print, so my father drew up his own carriage and wagon lists.

In the 'fifties, the steam railway was a curious mixture of friendliness and aloofness as far as the enthusiast was concerned. I often wondered why, as the manager, A M Sheard, had been very helpful to many enthusiasts in the 1930s. At last, we discovered the answer; shortly after the war, an enthusiast 'acquired' one of the single line train staffs, and 'AM' who was a very forceful character, put up the shutters.

It took many years to become accepted, and to explore the hidden world of the IMR, and in this book, I have included not just the steam trains of the IMR, and the electric stock of the MER, but the activities behind the scenes. One of the rarest scenes depicts the three-storey goods warehouse at Douglas. Few enthusiasts knew it

existed, let alone got into the place!

By the 'fifties, the Manx Electric Railway was in parlous condition, and at the prompting of Deemster Sir Percy Cowley (who was a friend of my grandmother) and Sir Charles Kerruish (Speaker of the House of Keys), it was taken into government ownership. By the 'sixties, the fate of the steam railway was balanced on a knife edge. From 1967 onwards, my father became increasingly involved in the campaign to keep the railway in being. I recall one senior government officer handing him a copy of a top secret government report, which had yet to be laid before Tynwald (ie the Manx parliament). Had he mishandled the situation, the results would have been catastrophic. Instead the flaws in the pro-closure case were analysed in devastating detail, ready to emerge the moment the report was published, and before it had gained acceptance. It was rejected by Tynwald. Little of the real story of those years has been made public. Even today, there is much that cannot be told, but I have lifted the veil in a few places.

The Isle of Man Railway Company itself used the abbreviations IOMR and IMR. For consistency, I have opted to use IMR throughout this book.

ACKNOWLEDGEMENTS

My father and I longed to do a colour book on the fascinating railways of the Isle of Man, but until I met Tom Ferris and Chris Salter of Midland Publishing, it remained a pipe dream. Tom and Chris had sufficient faith in the project to say 'go ahead', and my first acknowledgement is to them. Sadly my father passed away a year before I met Tom and Chris, so he was never to see this book, but it is as much his book as mine. It contains many of his photographs, and his enthusiasm

sparked my own as a child. My mother supported and encouraged us in recording the railways, and in campaigning for them, and used her own camera to good effect also. Some of her views appear.

A friend, Tony Baxter, visited the Island in 1949, with colour film in his camera, and took some of the earliest known colour views of the IMR, which open our portrait of the steam railway.

My remaining acknowledgement is an immense one. It is to the directors,

officers and men of the steam and electric railways, whose friendship we cherished, and without whose skill and dedication, the railways would not have survived.

This book is respectfully dedicated to the memory of my father, Dr Robert Preston Hendry, MRCS, LRCP, BA(Cantab), FBMA, RAMC (Retd).

Robert Hendry
Rugby, February 1993

INTRODUCTION

If one is to understand the railways of the Isle of Man, a sketch of the Island is useful. 'The Island', is located in the Irish sea, and is approximately 33 miles long by 11 miles broad, with an area of 227 square miles. The population stood at about 50,000 from the 1870s to the 1970s. Half of the population resided in the Douglas area. Much of the central area consists of high ground, bisected by the low lying valleys of the Dhoo and Neb, which provided an east west access between Douglas and Peel. The terrain dictated the routes the steam and electric lines would follow.

The Island came under Scottish, English and Viking influence, and the indigenous population is of mixed Celtic and Norse origin, and this is reflected in the place names. Although part of the British Isles, it is not part of the United Kingdom, having its own Parliament, Tynwald, and elected assembly, the House of Keys. The British Crown appoints a Lieutenant-Governor.

Traditional industries included farming and fishing, with lead and silver mining at Laxey and Foxdale. Tourism developed in Victorian times, and by 1914, half a million visitors flocked to the Island each year. The railways drew support from and nurtured the tourist trade.

Top: **The railway still provided an all-year service, and this included school trains between Douglas and Peel. No 12 *Hutchinson* is ready to depart with such a turn in April 1959**

Centre: **Until 1927, the Douglas horse-trams provided an all-year service, and apart from the familiar open 'toast-rack' cars, a few single deck cars were acquired. In modern times, their appearances were confined to rainy days, so the chance to photograph No 1 on a glorious August day in 1959 was welcome. My first forays behind the lens, instead of in front of it were the following year.**

Bottom: **My father captured Snaefell No 6 just below the Bungalow in June 1963. By this time, I was filming too, but had learnt to keep clear of his line, or go to ground. The dark object in the grass shows it was the latter choice on this occasion!**

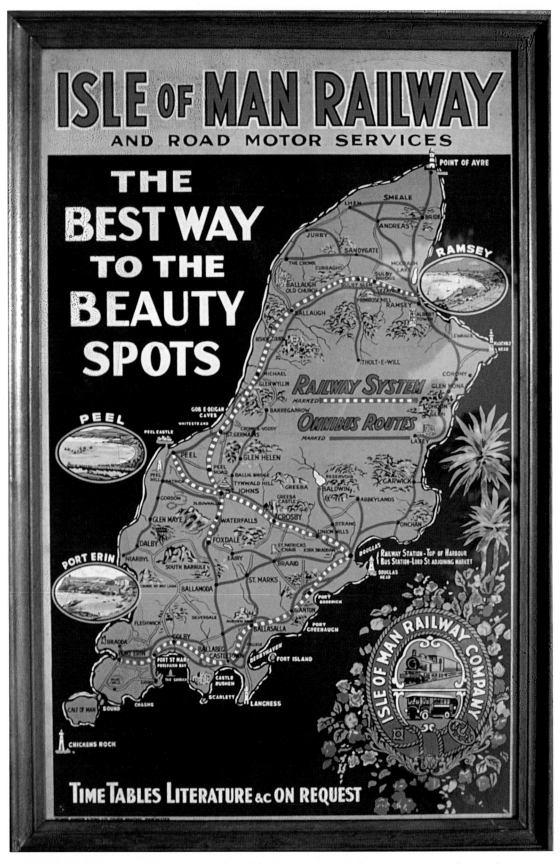

From Edwardian times, the IMR produced colourful map-posters, and when bus operations began, these included the road services as well. This map shows the network at the start of the thirties, and supplies were doled out so sparingly, that it was still in use after the war, even though the Foxdale line had shut by then!

Chapter One

THE ISLE OF MAN

RAILWAY

The Isle of Man Railway Company was founded in 1870 to build lines from Douglas to Peel in the west, Castletown, Port St Mary and Port Erin in the south, and Ramsey in the north. Fund raising was slow, and the Ramsey line was dropped. Even so, mainland financiers had to be brought in to raise enough funds. The 11½ mile Douglas-Peel line opened on 1st July 1873, and the 15½ mile Port Erin line on 1st August 1874.

The demise of the Ramsey proposal prompted the formation of a fresh company, The Manx Northern Railway, in 1877. Owing to the formidable terrain north of Douglas, a west coast route, diverging from the IMRCo Peel line at St Johns was selected, and the 16½ mile line opened on 23rd September 1879.

The Foxdale mines, 2½ miles south of St John's were some of the most prosperous lead and silver mines in the British Isles, and with the backing of the mining company, the Manx Northern interests proposed a branch line, to be built by a third concern, the Foxdale Railway. This opened in August 1886 .

The collapse of Dumbell's Bank in 1900 caused a financial panic on the Island, and the MNR was unable to persuade the Isle of Man Bank to renew its debenture bonds, and by 1903 had to agree to the sale of its line to its more prosperous neighbour, the IMR. The necessary Act was passed in 1904.

Bus competition began in the 1920s, but under its newly appointed manager, A M Sheard, the railway defeated and bought out its bus competitors, and ran an integrated road and rail service for almost forty years.

When Tony Baxter visited Douglas station in 1949, a few engines still carried the dark green livery introduced when the line opened in 1873. No 8 *Fenella* of 1894 was little altered from the day she arrived on the Island, save for vacuum brakes and Ross 'pop' valves. Cattle trains were still a regular sight. This view is taken from a rare addition-screen process glass slide.

MR SHEARD'S RAILWAY

Below left: **A new 'Indian Red' livery had been adopted by A M Sheard shortly after the war. Tony Baxter caught No 4 *Loch* in the new colour scheme during his 1949** visit to Douglas station. Originally a small boilered engine, she received a larger boiler in 1909, and retained Salter valves until her 1968 rebuild.

Below right: **No 10 *G H Wood* had received** a new boiler the year prior to Tony's visit, and also carried the Indian Red livery.

Bottom: **No 16 *Mannin* of 1926, the last engine bought by the IMR, was still in** dark green, and save for the loss of chimney numerals, in original condition in 1949.

The views on this page are also reproduced from 2¼x2¼in addition-screen glass slides.

Top: **In the 'fifties, Douglas was still a busy station, and on a good day, 60 or 70 coaches were needed for traffic (out of a total of 75 bogie carriages). Four engines on shed, preparing for the morning exodus of holidaymakers was a common sight.**

Above: **By 1959, money was tight, and although a new boiler had come for No 11 *Maitland*, other engines limped on from year to year. No 6 *Peveril*, caught at Douglas on a glorious August afternoon, was nearing the end of her career.**

Top: **Some of the original 1873 four wheel carriages, mounted in pairs on bogie chassis, and painted in a utility brown livery, were set aside for the 'schools' workings, which continued on the Peel line until the early 'sixties.**

Above: **A vivid 'red and cream' livery was adopted after the War, and freshly overhauled stock made an eye-catching sight, as with F30, a 3rd saloon dating from 1905.**

Left: **By the early 'sixties, Nos 3, 4, 6 and 9 had been put in store, and with an intensive service, the surviving engines were putting in a high mileage, with tight turn-round times. Cleaning was perforce neglected, and No 10 *G H Wood,* seen on 20th May 1961, was the worst affected.**

Above: **On 31st December 1959, the County Donegal Railways Joint Committee closed down, and when its stock was auctioned in 1961, Donald Shaw, the IMR loco superintendent, was able to buy the two most modern diesel railcars, Nos 19 and 20, dating from 1950/51. They entered service on the IMR in 1961, and were useful in cutting winter running bills. Shortage of luggage space persuaded the IMR to adapt goods van G19 to run between the cars in winter, and we see the ensemble at St John's in November 1963.**

Right: **1963 saw the disappearance of an IMR 'Institution'. In the 'twenties, the company had tried a two-tone brown paint scheme based upon the Lancashire & Yorkshire Railway livery. The last vehicle to carry it was E5, one of the 1870s passenger brake vans. She was used as a stores van at the foot of the Port Erin departure platform at Douglas for decades, but vanished out of sight during tidying up prior to a Royal trip by the Queen Mother in 1963.**

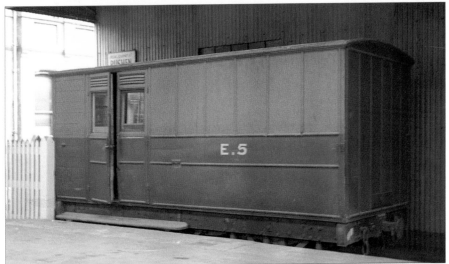

Bottom: **Railway histories abound with references to 'the Board Room'. Few readers will have been inside the IMR board room let alone had the opportunity to photograph there. By the early 'sixties, there was considerable anxiety as to the future of the railway at Board level.**

IOM ROAD SERVICES

Some of the published accounts of the Isle of Man Railway suggest that the IMR involvement with buses had weakened the railway. In fact, the reverse was the case. Every accounting device which A M Sheard could use to allocate expenses to the buses, or revenues to the railway side was seized upon, and by 1960, the buses, with their railway inspired 'device' (right) were vital in keeping the trains running. Today this would be called 'creative accounting'.

Between 1945 and 1950, 'AM' added fifty new buses to the fleet, This big influx, topped up by occasional deliveries in the late 'fifties and early 'sixties, gave Sheard the resources to keep his bus and rail empire running. The Road Services was technically a private subsidiary of the IMR, but questions about the bus side were discouraged by the comment that 'any information might be of value to potential competitors'. The real reason, known only to 'AM' and a handful of senior officers, was that it was only through massive infusions of bus money that the railway was kept alive, and that bus revenue and costs were correspondingly distorted.

Left: Bus competition had began in 1927 with a mainland backed concern, *Manxland*. In 1928, the railway introduced its own Thorneycroft buses, which outclassed the opposition, and after a brief but ruthless battle, in which A M Sheard and his officers were ready to outrun and undercut any move by their rivals, *Manxland* and another concern *Manx Motors,* came under railway control. The 1928 Thorneycrofts ran until the late 1940s, and 'AM' kept one allegedly for works duties. IOM Road Services No 13 is descending Slieu Lewaigue en route to Ramsey in 1969.

Centre left: With three fleets dating from 1927-28, few new buses were added, but by 1945, age and war use had taken its toll, and six Bedford 'Utility' OWB single deckers were acquired. When the only independent bus operator outside Douglas was taken over in 1950, another OWB joined the fleet. This was FMN 934, new to J Broadbent of Ramsey in 1945. She became No 86 in the IMRS fleet, later 119, and was withdrawn in 1966.

Centre right: When she arrived on the Island in 1946, Road Services No 3, a Leyland Titan PD1, created a furore, for Manx law prohibited the carriage of more than 34 seated passengers outside Douglas. With postwar shortages of materials, UK government policy was to encourage the production of double rather than single deckers. The greater carrying capacity of double deckers made better use of resources. Sheard was offered early delivery of double deckers, or a long wait for single deckers, and realised that if he ran a 56-seat double decker, with 22 upper deck seats roped off, he would comply with the law, and make the authorities look so foolish that a change in the law was inevitable. No 3 is seen at Ramsey on 23rd August 1969, her 34-seat period only a dim memory!

Bottom left: The revolutionary Leyland Olympic HR40 integral single deckers were added in the late '40s. Road Services No 49 had clocked up 20 years of service when she was caught at Laxey in 1970.

FREIGHT SERVICES

Right: **No 24 (later 111), a 1948 Morris Commercial 45/55cwt platform lorry, was being loaded from goods van G15 at the freight depot at Ramsey on 3rd June 1963 in a scene which epitomises traditional freight handling methods.**

Centre: As freight traffic waned, the old cattle wagon washing siding at the back of Douglas carriage shed became the scrap road. This was the scene, 13th April 1963, with K2, K1, K7, G2, K6, K18 and K16 awaiting their fate. The third vehicle, K7 is an open topped ex MNR cattle wagon.

Bottom: **By the early 'sixties, many wagons had been broken up, but bolster wagons L1 and L2 were still available for timber, steel, or other long loads. The decline in freight traffic had resulted in some of the older lorries being laid up, including the Ford in the background.**

Below: **Apart from a modest stone goods shed at the bottom of the yard, freight facilities at Douglas included a 3-storey freight warehouse, which backed onto the head offices. As the company's need for storage space declined, it was leased to Spillers, and then fell into disuse. Few enthusiasts knew of its existence, but it was to become familiar territory to my father and I. In the early 'seventies, the then manager, Bill Lambden, invited us to explore the lofts, as he believed that a good deal of paperwork had been stored there and feared that it would otherwise be lost. Tickets, timetables, posters, letters, drawings and a host of other items came to light, adding a new dimension to the history of the IMR.**

THE END OF AN ERA

In the 'sixties, we knew nothing of the covert efforts made by Sheard to keep the wheels turning. 'AM' died, appropriately still in harness in 1965, and his successor, Bill Lambden, was a well known bus and coach journalist, and light railway enthusiast. One wondered how the change would affect the railway.

At the end of the summer, Bill Lambden started to look at the figures, for the bus operating data did not make any sense to him, and as he unravelled the labyrinth, he discovered the extent to which the railway was dependent upon transfusions from the buses, and more worrying, the fall in bus profits. All rail services ceased in November 1965. It was a fraught period. Before seeing what happened, we will take a trip around the system.

Below left: **By 1963, the Ramsey line had only a service during the summer months and No 12 *Hutchinson* is depicted with the last train of the season, pulling away from Kirk Michael on a cold dreary September afternoon.**

Bottom: **This was a difficult time for the IMR though the bustle at St John's as late as 30th August 1965, was reassuring.**

Below right: **In 1966 the archaic slotted post signal at St John's lay idle and the signal box windows were boarded up.**

DOUGLAS

We will go back to the 'fifties and 'sixties, and journey from Douglas to Peel. Our first impression of Douglas station was the spacious booking hall with its impressive system map, which still showed the Foxdale line, thirty years after trains last ran there.

Walking down the platform, we might see a Peel train coming in, in this case No 5 *Mona* is entering the station on 17th August 1962, with a classic 2-coach train, comprising a half-brake and a guard coach (with five passenger compartments and one for the guard).

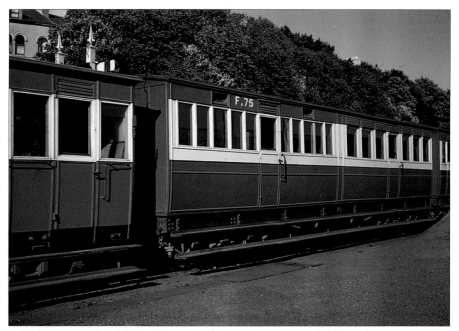

Above: **The Peel line had opened in 1873, the first train being hauled by No 1 *Sutherland*. 90 years later, she was still occasionally steamed, and when caught in Douglas shed on 4th September 1964 was cooling down after stand-by duty with the Ambulance train for the Manx Grand Prix races, for prior to the days of helicopters, the railway made an engine and van available in the event of injury to a rider in the TT or MGP races.**

Above right **A special 4-wheel saloon coach, A12, had been delivered in time for the opening and was used by the chairman, the Duke of Sutherland, the Governor, Sir Henry Loch and other VIPs. United with another 4-wheeler, C9, on a bogie frame, it became F75, and is portrayed, as the far half of F75, in traffic in August 1959.**

Right: **In Victorian days. the IMR had used a dark blue buttoned upholstery in its 1st class stock. This was later replaced by a blue and gold patterned cloth, but the old style survived in F75, as did one of the folding tables. A second table had been transferred to the other part of the coach.**

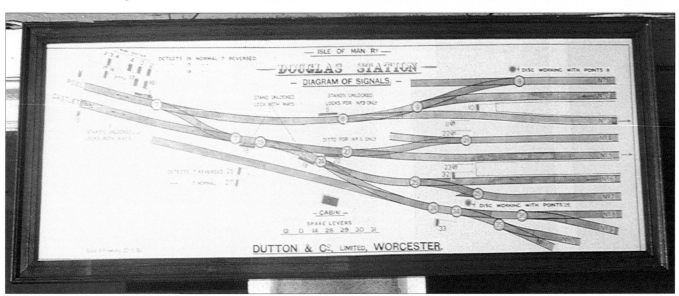

Facing page bottom: **The original Douglas station was swept away in a dramatic reconstruction in the late 1880s and early 1890s, and by November 1891, when discussions began with Dutton & Co of Worcester over new signalling, most of the new trackage was in situ. From the outset, the project was bedevilled by differences between Dutton himself and the firm's London agent, J P O'Donnell, who was soon to form his own company, Evans, O'Donnell.**

Right: **The installation was completed in 1892, and included an imposing bracket signal at the station throat. One legacy of the Dutton - O'Donnell feud was the freakish way in which the home signals were arranged. Instead of separate levers for what would normally be 'outer homes', the outer signals were in fact merely repeaters for the inner homes.**

Below: **Douglas was one of the few locations ever to receive Dutton's patented 'Spring Handle' frame. Instead of a separate catch handle, the lever handle is pivoted, and locks the lever normal or pulled. The drawback is that accidental contact with the handle may cause the pulled lever to fly back, so securing latches are needed on point levers.**

ON SUNDAYS ONLY

Above: **The first station on the Peel line was Braddan, which was normally only open on a Sunday morning! Open air services were held at a nearby church, and large crowds were attracted to this novel form of worship in summer. A train would run out from Douglas, unload at Braddan, and then run on to Union Mills where the engine would run round and return to Douglas for a second special.**

Left: **The oval red target on No 12 *Hutchinson* is the IMR indication 'Special following in opposite direction' as the next train would be the second special hauled by No 12. After the second special, which was also run round at Union Mills, the engine would return to Braddan with the combined train, where it would uncouple from the train - in respect to the Lord - for the duration of the service, and then take the crowds back to Douglas. On this occasion, 23rd August 1964, the diesels were also pressed into use.**

CROSBY

Above: **Crosby station, with its chalet type building, typified the original Peel line stations, and indeed the first buildings at Douglas and Peel were also to this pattern. Trains continued to cross here to the end of services.**

Right: **No 10 *G H Wood* enters Crosby with a Peel train in August 1959, her grimy condition evidence of how hard the dwindling number of engines were being worked. The corrugated iron structure to the left is the goods shed.**

Top: **Entry to St John's station was controlled by a signal cabin built at MNR expense when the Northern line appeared. From late Victorian times, British practice has been to place running signals controlling a junction on a bracket, rather than above one another, but the old arrangement survived at St John's.**

Above: **Peel station was on a delightful harbourside location, with the town rising up behind it. The old buildings were replaced in Edwardian times by commodious masonry structures.**

Left: **No 16** *Mannin* **simmers between duties at Peel on 28th August 1963, her career almost at an end. The wooden shed to the right is the enginemens' bothy.**

THE SOUTH LINE

Right: **The Port Erin line opened on 1st August 1874, and as traffic soared, the original Douglas station soon became hopelessly inadequate. It was not until 1887 that complete reconstruction got under way, with a new office block, goods depot, loco shed and works, carriage shed** and station buildings. The new station, designed by a leading Manx architect, James Cowle, was a handsome structure in Ruabon brick. It opened in time for the 1892 season. In 1909, station canopies were added by Hill & Smith of Brierley Hill, in the West Midlands. The station had hardly altered by 1966.

Above centre: **The inner faces of the two long platforms were used for arrivals, and the outer faces for departures. No 13** *Kissack* **makes a spirited departure with an LRTL Special on 20th May 1961.**

Above: **Some Port Erin trains did depart from the centre road, and this was particularly useful when a banker was needed, as it could be attached on to the train via the engine escape road. On the** south line trains faced a long 1 in 65 to 1 in 70 climb out of Douglas, a hard task for an engine starting from cold. No 1 *Sutherland* is about to bank a Port Erin train in August 1959.

23

Top: **With five coaches and a few wagons, No 16 *Mannin* did not really need a banker on this August day in 1959, but as No 1 *Sutherland* had been steamed for heavy trains earlier in the day, she gave a friendly shove past the White Hoe Hospital.**

Centre: ***Sutherland* banks the train seen in the previous plate over the stone arch at Kewaigue. The grade eases half a mile short of Port Soderick, and the banker would drop off and run back light. If the engine had been coupled, the fireman would edge his way along the tank-side as the train was in motion, then along the running plate above the cylinders, and unhook in motion!**

Left: **Port Soderick was served by the steam railway, by launches from Douglas, and by the Marine Drive trams until 1939. It was a very popular resort, and a commodious station building was erected, much of the ground floor being given over to refreshment rooms.**

Below: Ballasalla was the first wayside community of any size, and the original 1870s station building survived until the mid 1980s, when it was removed at the behest of property developers. The red wooden shed to the right is the goods store, which had come from the First World War Knockaloe Alien Internment Camp near Peel. A capacious cattle dock testifies to the importance of the Ballasalla market in earlier times.

Above: No 16 *Mannin* makes an energetic departure from Ballasalla in 1959. The dark Indian Red engines, vivid red and cream coach livery, and grey wagons created an eye-catching ensemble. In later years, as the coach red became an ever duller shade, and the cream was tinged with green, it lost its charm, and the 1870s livery was eventually re-adopted, but in its heyday, AM's 1950s style was delightful.

Above: **It is August 1965, and as fireman Dicky Shimmin looks back to see all is well, a freshly repainted No 12** *Hutchinson* **pulls away from Port St Mary with less than half a mile of the journey left. The shade of No 12 is quite markedly different from that of No 16 on page 25.**

Left: **By 1963, train mileage had been cut back, and from being shabby, No 10** *G H Wood* **became immaculate. She is in the bay platform at Port Erin, just short of the pedestrian crossing which bisects the station and also the platform.**

Bottom: **I could not resist this traditional scene with a rake of wagons attached to the train, particularly as it was taken as late as 1978, at the start of government ownership. F39, the coach to the left, is the former 'Foxdale Coach', then in red and cream livery.**

THE RAMSEY LINE

The Ramsey line diverged from the Douglas - Peel line at St John's. Train workings were often fascinating, as we shall see in the next three plates, taken in the space of a few minutes on 3rd June 1963, the first day of the seasonal Ramsey service.

Right: **No 8 *Fenella* has piloted the combined 10.25am ex Douglas for Peel and Ramsey, and the crew have uncoupled in motion, and run on ahead of the train. The home signal for the Ramsey line is lowered at the extreme left.**

Centre: **The train engine has brought the combined train to a stand, the rear two coaches have been uncoupled and left on the main line, and the Peel portion run on into the station. No 8 is setting back on to the Ramsey portion, and the signalman already has the incoming signal lowered again, so that *Fenella* can run forward with her portion!**

Bottom: **The Peel** (left) **and Ramsey** (right) **portions await departure time in their respective platforms at St John's.**

Above: **My mother, Elaine Hendry, photographed this delightful panorama of St John's station in August 1965. No 5 *Mona* waits with a Ramsey service, whilst F27, one of two bogie luggage vans (nicknamed Empress Vans as they were delivered in Queen Victoria's jubilee year, 1897) lies in the yard.**

Left: **The then ill-kempt No 10 *G H Wood* heads a short Ramsey train across the level crossings past the site of the MNR station yard at St John's in August 1959. The Foxdale branch diverged from the Ramsey line a little further out, and climbed over the IMR on a tall arch east of the station.**

Bottom: **Poortown station opened on 18th June 1883, but was soon renamed Peel Road, and at the expense of a considerable walk, saved the journey into St John's and down to Peel. It had hardly altered by 1963.**

Top: **At Glen Mooar, the railway was carried across a deep ravine by means of a three span viaduct. The original 1879 MNR bridge was life expired by the start of the 1920s, and a replacement provided in 1921.**

Above: **With the many vantage points along the TT Course, 'Race' specials were a useful source of revenue. No 11** *Maitland* **heads the last ever north-bound Race special over Glen Mooar viaduct on 5th September 1968.**

AROUND 'MICHAEL

Above: **As well as running steam trains and buses, the IMR operated motor boats and even children's slides. It was a very innovative company!**

Above left: **Just south of Kirk Michael, the line crossed over Glen Wyllin, and the original MNR structure here was replaced by a plate girder bridge in 1915. Glen Wyllin had long been a popular resort and it was taken into railway ownership in the 1930s, and developed as a major attraction, with a cafe, boating lake, tennis, golf and a children's playground. No 8 *Fenella* heads a three coach train into Kirk Michael.**

Centre: **The Glen brought vast crowds to Kirk Michael, and at train time in summer, this otherwise quiet country station presented an animated appearance, as was the case in August 1959. The red sandstone buildings were characteristic of the wayside stations on the Manx Northern.**

Left: **The MNR crossed numerous roads, and unlike the IMR who frequently provided nothing more than a sentry box for the crossing keeper, the MNR built substantial cottages. This is Orrisdale No 1 crossing north of Kirk Michael. Although the signal is in the garden of the crossing lodge, it does NOT protect these gates, but the next crossing, Orrisdale No 2!**

RAMSEY

Top: **No 8 *Fenella* enters Ramsey station on 27th August 1959.** The station was on the north side of the town, and surrounded by open ground. Even the Great Western could not have eclipsed the 'off' given by the home signal!

Above: **It is 3rd June 1963, and *Fenella* drifts past the cattle dock at Ramsey en route to take water.** The Ramsey cattle market was another important source of traffic until the 1950s.

Right: **By August 1960, when K6 was photographed at Ramsey with the water tank and carriage shed in the background, it was rare to see a cattle wagon in use.**

Above: **As befitted the one-time head-quarters of the Manx Northern Railway, the station buildings at Ramsey were a sizeable structure, and as late as August 1961 were well kept. Today an industrial estate occupies the site.**

Left: **The last really long train we saw on the Ramsey line was on 14th August 1965, when the usual two coach working was strengthened to ten carriages for troop movements from a summer training camp.** *Fenella* **and** *Maitland* **pull away from bay platform at Ramsey.**

Below: **In order not to double head over the Glen Wyllin and Glen Mooar viaducts, No 8 ran round the train at Kirk Michael and banked it to St John's. After a helping push as far as the summit at Ballacurry on the way to Douglas, she returned to St John's to take another train.**

THE FOXDALE RAILWAY

Above: **The Foxdale branch climbed over the IMR Douglas line east of St John's station, near the junction with the ballast pit siding. The water tank to the left was supplied from the Foxdale Railway formation, and topped up the St John's station tanks.**

Right: **The ballast pit siding, off the Peel line, met the railway's needs, and sand and gravel were also sold. It is an all but forgotten part of the IMR.**

Far right: **The Foxdale line had been ballasted with waste from the Mines spoil heaps. Although passenger services had ended in 1940, and freight workings in 1944, the high lead content in the ballast kept the weeds at bay as late as October 1974, just a few months before lifting.**

Bottom: **The Foxdale Railway was carried over the highway between Lower and Upper Foxdale, and the IMR used the plate bridge as an advert for its 5 shillings (25p) 2-day 'GO AS YOU PLEASE' tickets in the 1930s. The advert was still there in September 1964.**

Left: **From November 1965, the steam railway lay idle, and during the winter and spring of 1966, the IMRCo carried out a thorough examination under its new manager, Bill Lambden. Gradually it became clear how heavily the railway was dependent upon bus operations. Meanwhile an IOM government Transport Commission was also at work, but whilst the parties deliberated, it was a worrying time for enthusiasts, and as the grass encroached upon the three foot metals at Glen Mooar and a host of other places, one wondered if the trains would ever run again.**

Bottom left: **The massive restocking of the bus fleet in 1945-52 had staved off ill-times, but by the mid 'sixties, many of these vehicles were ageing, including the four Leyland Tiger PS1 single deckers with Eastern Coach works bodies, a most unusual combination. IMRS 34 is depicted in Port Erin garage. Today the structure houses the Railway Museum. Happily, No 34 is privately preserved.**

Centre: **Seven Dennis Falcon 30-seat single-deckers arrived second-hand ex Aldershot & District to replace the venerable Second World War Bedford OWBs. Some, including IMRS 29, seen at Maughold on 17th August 1967, entered service in Aldershot & District green with ROAD SERVICES on a red rectangle.**

Below: **Although bus operations were becoming unprofitable, Bill Lambden felt that coach services had a future, and three luxurious Leyland Leopards with Duple bodies entered service in 1968. No 35 is seen at Lord Street bus station the following summer.**

THE RAILWAY REVIVED

Above right: **Suddenly the future looked more promising, when the Marquess of Ailsa took a lease on the railway. A special trip was organised on Sunday 28th May 1967, using the diesel railcars to visit Peel and Kirk Michael.**

Bottom: **The day after the diesel trip, Monday 29th May, dawned fine, and soon No 11 *Maitland* was hard at work shunting carriages in Douglas station yard. She was in a striking new 'spring green' livery, and it was a thrill to see the railway back at work.**

Centre: **Sir Philip Wombwell, Bt, who was managing the venture for Lord Ailsa, had planned a dramatic re-opening, and as a retired military man, wisely decided upon a training exercise, the 'dress rehearsal' for Thursday 1st June. A cavalcade of locos was to proceed down the loco escape road at Douglas, and Philip is positioning No 12 *Hutchinson*. By now the engines carried a new crest which included a depiction of *Mannin* in green livery. (Top left)**

Right: **The new transfers for the side tanks had arrived in the charge of two well known clergymen. The first IMR engine to carry the new light green livery was less than three inches long. It was a 4mm model owned by the Rev Teddy Boston. He suggested the idea to Sir Philip, and the rest is history! No 8 *Fenella* looks a treat in the new livery at Douglas during the dress rehearsal.**

Centre: **The action now switches to Peel station. A directors special and three public trains, A, B and C were planned, so that Peel would host four engines and twenty seven carriages! No 11 is sitting on the stock of train A in the carriage siding, No 8 is arriving with train B and 10 is watering.**

Below: **Railway enthusiasts fall into two groups, those who knew Teddy Boston, and those who did not. Teddy was a delightful and warm-hearted character, and trips lightly across the growing flood coming from some time expired Fire Brigade hoses at Peel. Teddy's lifelong friend, Rev Wilbur Awdry, of 'Thomas the Tank' fame, was acting as guard on one train. The rule book said to screw down the brakes on the fall from St John's to Peel. He did so, but the brake was rather worn to start with, and with well watered rails at Peel, the train only just pulled up in time!**

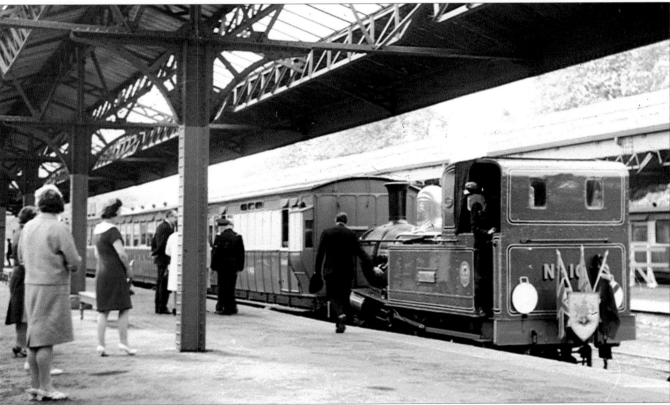

Top: **Lord Ailsa's family arrived on the island on the 2nd June and were taken from Ronaldsway Airport to Douglas by special train headed by No 11. When my father and I went to inspect the site the previous evening, the sign board had not yet arrived!**

Above: **As No 11 *Maitland* pulled into Douglas, Sir Philip Wombwell hurried down the platform to welcome the Marquess formally.**

Left: **Pipers were on hand to add a suitable Scottish flavour to the proceedings, for the Ailsa family seat is in South West Scotland.**

Above: **Alas the glorious weather broke on Friday evening, and Saturday 3rd June dawned damp and grey. However, the damp atmosphere provided a dramatic action study of No 11 leaving Douglas with the re-opening special. The leading coach, F75, had been used by the Duke of Sutherland when the line was opened in 1873.**

Left: **No 15 *Caledonia*, colloquially 'The Cale'. was station pilot at Douglas on 3rd June. She was the only 6-coupled engine owned by the IMR, and was built by Dübs of Glasgow for the Manx Northern Railway in 1885. *Caledonia* was No 4 on the MNR and was renumbered on the amalgamation of the two companies.**

Above: **It was wonderful to see the railway back in business in 1967, for we had wondered if we would ever see No 8 running round at Peel, or any of the other myriad of familiar scenes.**

Right: **The Peel line reopened on 3rd June 1967, the Ramsey line the following day, and the south line followed as far as Castletown. Beyond Castletown, the line was affected by a utility main being laid in, so was unavailable. Sir Philip made valiant efforts to attract freight to the railway, and this led to some unusual workings. Traditionally, freight stock had always been marshalled at the rear of trains, but when a G van had to be worked from Ballasalla to Douglas on 2nd September 1967, it was added at the head of the train.**

FREIGHT TRAFFIC

Below: A container ship service had commenced running to Castletown, and in the winter of 1967-68, Sir Philip secured the contract to move containers by rail between Castletown and Douglas. Eleven of the Pairs coaches (the 1873-74 4-wheelers mounted in pairs on bogie chassis) were stripped to provide flat wagons, one being further modified as a

bogie well wagon. No 10 *G H Wood* heads through Santon on 17th April 1968 with a container freight, the leading vehicle being an ex-MNR G-van, and the second vehicle the bogie well wagon.

Bottom left: IMR rolling stock had always been distinguished by letter codes, indicating the type of vehicle: A-F for coaching stock, G - goods vans, H - drop door opens, K - cattle, L - bolsters, M - drop side opens. In traditional style, the bogie flats were given a letter code, and R5

sits with an IOM Ferry express container at Castletown on 19th April 1968. The wooden canopy screen to the Castletown buildings was alas demolished in the winter of 1992-93.

Bottom right: The railway acquired its own cleverly named 'MAN-TAINORs', but the venture was not a success financially, and ended soon after these scenes were recorded.

CALEDONIA

Below: **After a season in light green, *Caledonia* was restored to MNR red, and was fresh from the paint-shop when photographed on 28th May 1968.**

Bottom: **On 2nd June 1968, she headed a special from Douglas to St John's for the Isle of Man Steam Railway Supporters Association. One of the photo stops was at Union Mills.**

Top left: **With so many engines laid up for boiler repairs, Philip Wombwell was concerned about motive power, and Lord Ailsa agreed that two new boilers should be ordered from Hunslet of Leeds. The first boiler was to go into No 4 *Loch,* and by 28th May 1968, the boiler was in the fitting shop at Douglas.**

Top right: **This is the only occasion on which we saw eight IMR engines in motion at St Johns. Several of the stored engines had been put on display at St John's, and were shunted into the carriage shed each evening. No 5 is shunting 15, 16, 6, 1 and 14 as 11 and 12 head the 4.34pm ex Peel to Douglas train.**

Above: **By 6th September 1968, the IMR workshops, under the locomotive superintendent, Donald Shaw, had completed the re-boilering of No 4 *Loch,* and she sat resplendent in the sun.**

Top: **There were dark clouds on the horizon, for losses had been far heavier than expected in 1967-68, and the railway was again in jeopardy. As driver John Elkin oiled round No 12 *Hutchinson* at Ramsey on the last day of scheduled services, 6th September, it looked as if it was farewell to the Ramsey line.**

Above: **The Peel and Port Erin lines were due to close the following day, but by this time, No 4 was ready for service, and she ran out light to St John's to shunt the engines out of the carriage shed under the supervision of Donald Shaw. Donald had joined the railway at the start of the 'twenties, became loco superintendent in 1946, and remained in harness until 1975. Without his down-to-earth practical know-how, the railway could not have survived.**

Left: **It can seldom have occurred that a locomotive re-entered service on the day the line closed down, but No 4 *Loch* took her maiden trip on the 10.24am ex Peel on Saturday, 7th September 1968.**

ANOTHER CLOSURE AND ANOTHER REPRIEVE

Opposite page top: **A few hours later, we returned to Peel to photograph a sister engine No 5 *Mona* waiting for the last passenger working from Peel. The 'Douglas or Bust' headboard caused considerable offence to some of the older, more traditional railwaymen.**

Opposite page, centre: **A few days later, I chanced to meet Driver Elkin in Ramsey, and he told me that one of the oil specials was running, taking fuel between the IOM Electricity Board plants at Peel and Milntown, on the outskirts of Ramsey. This service, which began in the late summer continued for 2-3 weeks after the end of passenger workings, and provided a unique opportunity to photograph No 4 *Loch* on freight duty at Ramsey.**

Opposite page, bottom: **In 1969, Tynwald approved a £7,500 grant for each of the next three years to assist Lord Ailsa in running the south line, and services resumed to and from Port Erin. No 4 *Loch* drifts past the old Upholstery shops on the 10.12am from Port Erin on 12th September 1969.**

This page, top: **The Marquess had appointed Max Crookall as manager for the 1969-71 period, and Max worked hard to attract traffic. The Douglas carnival usually warranted a special train, and the nocturnal return journey to Port Erin was fascinating. No 4 *Loch* awaits time with the carnival special on 21st August 1969.**

Centre: **Few people realise that the IMR possessed not one, but two engines named *Mannin*! The lesser known *Mannin* was a wooden carnival float, originally built to sit on top of one of the railway's delivery vans, and later towed behind a tractor. A number of genuine loco fittings were used on the mock up, which trundles along Lord Street on 24th August 1972. Alas the second *Mannin* fell victim to woodworm a few years later, and was broken up.**

Right: **Spare stock was stabled in St John's carriage shed, and occasionally vehicles were switched. The last train we ever saw on the Peel line was near Ballacraine on 10th September 1970, when the CDR railcars were on weed clearance duty prior to a coach transfer trip a few days later.**

Top: **The Ailsa lease ended in 1972, and with a grant from the IOM Tourist Board, the IMRCo resumed operation. This included the Centenary special on Sunday 1st July 1973, with Nos 13 *Kissack* and 10 *G H Wood.* Although the centenary being celebrated was that of the Peel line the special ran on the south line.**

Centre left: **In the 1970s, my father founded the Isle of Man Railway Society. The Society's first help for the railway was a cheque for £200 towards rolling stock repairs. Appropriately this was presented to the railway on 1st August 1974, the centenary of the Port Erin line. From left to right are L T Bond, secretary of the IOM Tourist Board, and a valuable friend to the railways, Alex Davidson, Vice Chairman of the IMRCo, Dr Hendry, chairman of the Society, and Bill Lambden, general manager of the IMR and Road Services from 1965 to 1976.**

Centre right: **On the steam railway, funds were low. The smith, Eddie Quiggin, is repairing tools for the PW gang in 1974. The air blast for the smithy had been driven off the works shafting, which was quite costly to run, until one day, Eddie had a brain wave. His wife's old vacuum cleaner sucked in at one end, but blew out at the other, and the vacuum cleaner duly appeared in the smithy as an air pump!**

Bottom: **Funds remained tight on the bus side, and Bill Lambden made judicious purchases of second hand double deckers from Stratford Blue and Bournemouth. IOM Road Services No 74 was a Leyland Titan PD3/1, new to Bournemouth in 1963, and acquired by Bill 11 years later. She is near Greensill's corner on Douglas Promenade on 1st August 1974.**

Opposite page, top: **Some of the older staff stayed on long after retirement age, and one of the legendary engine men, Hughie Duff, stands beside No 10 *G H Wood,* as one of the temporary staff, Julian Edwards coals the locomotive. It is 31st July 1974, and the south line has completed a century of service.**

Opposite page, bottom: **On Centenary day, 1st August 1974, No 4 *Loch* was suitably beflagged, and is caught at Castletown. The flags include the Union Jack, the White ensign, the Scottish lion, and a green flag with a Union Jack and a harp, representing Ireland! This would have been fine for the Coronation of King George V before the First World War, when they had been purchased, but by the 1970s, Ireland had been partitioned for more than half a century, and the flag suited neither the north nor the south, but a trifle like that did not faze the Isle of Man Railway Company. The flags still had years of life left!**

LIFTING IN THE NORTH
THREATS IN THE SOUTH

Top left: The long sleep of the closed lines was to come to a close, and in 1974 the metalwork on the Peel, Ramsey and Foxdale lines were sold to Millen Metals of Belfast for £149,500, and the land sold to the IOM government. This scene, one of the saddest we ever took, was a farewell to the closed sections, as Millen's men tore up the Peel and Ramsey formation just west of St John's station.

Top right: The stock which lay on the abandoned sections was also sold to the scrap men, and by November 1975 this was all that remained of carriages F17 and N43.

Centre: The Tourist Board support was only for three years 1972-74, and by that autumn, the fate of the railway hung in the balance once more. The Licensed Victuallers National Homes Conference was being held in Douglas in October 1974, and special trains had been booked by the champagne firm of Moët & Chandon which ran after the end of scheduled services on the 8th, 9th and 10th October. No 13 *Kissack* storms past the White Hoe on the last of the specials.

Left: As a charity stunt, armed desperadoes were to hold up the returning specials at Santon, and a touch of the wild west came to the most tranquil of IMR stations in October 1974 as masked gunmen prepared to rob the train. They had already held a gun to the photographer's head! As there was some opposition in Tynwald to adequate funding of the railway, the future looked bleak, and it seemed not unlikely that the IMR would pass into history as the only railway whose trains had been held up by gunmen on the last day.

THE SHORT LINE

Top right: **The events of 1974-75 have never been told in full, but suffice it to say that the recommendation of no further support for the railway, which had been drafted by Tynwald's Steering Committee on Transport was rejected. The political will was not there for full operation of the south line, and in 1975, train services ran only between Port Erin and Castletown. At Douglas, spare stock lay silent and out of use, and a coating of rust covered the 3ft metals for much of 1975.**

Centre: **To provide an added attraction on the railway, the former IOM Road Services garage at Port Erin became a railway museum, and during construction work, and alterations the following winter, tracks snaked across the floor.**

Below right: **In 1975, the IOM Railway Society purchased N42 from the scrap merchants. She was moved by road from St John's to Ballasalla, and by rail to Port Erin. Donald Shaw, the IMR loco superintendent, invited my mother and I to travel in a coach with no windows, its doors tied on with string, and much of its woodwork missing. For reasons which eluded us, passers by seemed surprised at the sight of two people and a dog leaning out of the windows of such an interesting vehicle. Contrary to popular legend, the Cleminson coach rode exceptionally smoothly.**

Below: **Restoration work began on N42 in September 1975, and by 1976, she was resplendent in MNR livery in the Port Erin Railway museum.**

THE GOVERNMENT TAKES CHARGE

Left: The 'short line' was not a success, and train services resumed to Douglas in 1977. By this time, the political attitude had changed, and the railway was seen as a vital part of the tourist industry, and was taken into government ownership prior to the 1978 season. No 4 *Loch* in her new medium red livery, is on the hoist in the fitting shops, during August 1984.

Centre: Money was available for carriage repairs, and the last MNR bogie coach, F39, known as the 'Foxdale Coach' from its long sojourn on the branch, was selected for rebuilding. The new chief executive, Bill Jackson was discussing the project with us, and we suggested to him that as 1979 marked the centenary of the MNR, that it would be nice to see a coach in MNR livery once more, so F39 assumed the later MNR colours as MNR No 15. Apart from the pleasure of seeing a vehicle in Manx Northern colours, another blessing was that the railways had adopted a new livery with modern 'lower case' adhesive lettering, and when Bill Jackson discovered that the old time finish was very popular with passengers, he was shrewd enough to agree to other vehicles receiving the same treatment!

Bottom: The IMR 2-4-0Ts had originated from Beyer Peacock's Gorton works in Manchester, and the Manchester Museum of Science & Industry wanted to display a classic Beyer engine in their collection. No 3 *Pender*, one of the original 1873 engines was transferred to the Museum, and is seen prior to departure from Douglas.

BILL JACKSON
AT WORK

Above: **As well as being the Centenary of
the MNR, 1979 was the Millennium of
Tynwald, and a series of events took place.
Given the close associations between the
Island and the Vikings, it was appropriate
that King Olav V of Norway paid a visit to
the Island, and indeed travelled by special
train. We had visited Norway and found
that on their National day, trains carried
the Norwegian flag, and we suggested to
Bill Jackson that the train should be**
properly **decorated. On the day of the trip,
there was a flap as the only Norwegian
flag was in Ramsey. We hastily collected it,
and got it to the IMR just in time! The
Royal Train, headed by No 13** *Kissack*
draws into Douglas station.

Centre: **King Olav, who had been
reviewing a regatta at Port St Mary prior to
the Royal journey, leaves Douglas station.
J J Christian, the Chairman of the
Railways Board, is to the right, and Bill
Jackson, the Chief executive is just inside
the Booking Hall doors.**

Right: **The boilers of Nos 10** *G H Wood* **and
12** *Hutchinson* **were condemned, and new
boilers ordered from Israel Newton. The
first of these, for No 12, is seen in the
fitting shops in September 1980. The new
boilers were to a larger design, similar in
size to** *Mannin's* **1926 boiler.**

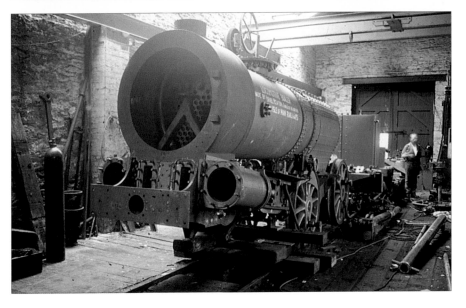

Top: **The rebuild proceeded during the winter of 1980-81 and No 12 made her trial trip, on 22nd May 1981, double heading a service train with No 13 *Kissack*. With two engines putting out plenty of steam and smoke it was a dramatic sight. To add diversity to the railway, No 12 had received a *'Mannin'* style cab and a dark blue livery, whilst 13 was in the old IMRCo deep green.**

Left: **Although the plan had been for No 10 *G H Wood* to receive the second new boiler, providing the railway with five steam locomotives, the boiler on No 11 was also giving trouble, and as less work was required, the new boiler was diverted to her. *Maitland* runs through the beautiful Crogga valley on a delightful spring day.**

WINTER STEAM

Opposite page, bottom right: **A public petition was circulated in the south of the Island, asking for a shoppers train on the steam railway, and a Fridays only service ran in the winter of 1980-81, and again the following winter. Steam heat fittings were refurbished on a number of carriages, and trains once again ran through the winter countryside. Peter Callister, acting for the day as guard, helps some of the shoppers on board at Castletown on 26th March 1982.**

Above: **No 12 *Hutchinson* pulls away from Douglas with the return train later that day. The bare trees in the background and crisp exhaust testify to the winter operation.**

Right: **Twenty years ago, one of the classic locations for photography was the bridge over the Silverburn river, just west of Castletown, but steady growth of the trees has made it increasingly difficult for the photographer. The chance of a winter train, with a glorious reflection in the still waters of the Silverburn was too good to miss. Again, the occasion was the 26th March 1982.**

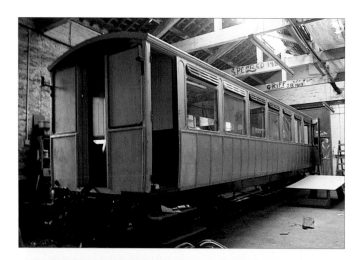

Top left: **Ever since the 1930s, money had been tight, and there was a backlog of repairs. Carriages received new cladding, and in 1984, three of the 1905 saloons were fitted with corridor connections to create the bar set, which could be hired by special parties. The date painted on the roof beams show that the workshops had not been repainted recently!**

Top right: **The buses had preceded the steam railway into public ownership, for in 1976, the Road Services and Douglas Corporation bus services were united**

under the government owned IOM National Transport. **This was later merged with the combined steam and electric railway organisation, as Isle of Man Passenger Transport. W854MAN was a Leyland Panther single decker, acquired from Preston in 1983, which ran until 1986. Few Panthers were built, and it was interesting to see such rare vehicles on the Island. At first numbered 81, she later became No 11. The Red and White livery was applied to a few IMR coaches as well, notably the bar set.**

Above: **Although there was a great deal of progress during Bill Jackson's time as Chief Executive, there were unfortunate losses too. One of the saddest was the sale of much of the Ballasalla station site to property developers in the 1980s. A modern office block sprouted in the goods yard, and the developers soon wanted the 1870s station buildings removed. A new station building appeared, but scenes such as No 11 *Maitland* taking water in 1982, with a traditional IMR backdrop are no more, since a somewhat mundane office block has replaced this lovely scene.**

Top: **Bill Jackson's successor, Robert Smith, formerly of London Transport, received an unusual request soon after he took over. The railway had been selected for filming purposes, and as the film included scenes on the Trans Siberian Railway, the film producers felt it would add to the authenticity if the engine were painted black. No 11 *Maitland* duly received an unlined black livery, which she retained for the 1989 season.**

Above left: **In 1974, the IOM Railway Society had rescued the 1893 IMR accident crane from scrap, and in 1990, the Department of Highways, Ports & Properties offered to restore the crane for display on the site of Union Mills station. The crane was moved to Douglas in 1990, and taken by road to the Highways Board depot at Crosby for rebuilding. The Gibbins crane is being lifted off railway metals by a former US Army Air Force Second World War 'Lorain' crane owned by Captain Stephen Carter.**

Above right: **The DHPP staff did a superb job in rebuilding the crane, and in May 1991. she was taken out to Union Mills by road. The highway is connected to the station by a narrow track, which ran down to the IMR cattle dock, and is known locally as the Bull Road. For part of the journey, rails were laid ahead of the crane, which was towed forward and the track behind taken up and moved ahead, a technique I had read of, but never expected to see!**

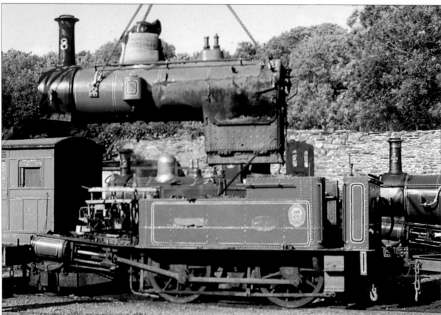

Left: **In the early years of government ownership, the IOM Railway Society purchased three of the stored locomotives, No 5 *Mona* of 1874, No 8 *Fenella* of 1894 and No 9 *Douglas* of 1896. The Society's plan was to return the engines to working order. No 8 was moved into the fitting shops in Douglas, where she is seen in September 1989, prior to the start of the £35,000 rebuild. When finished, it is hoped that she will run on the steam railway.**

Centre: **The boiler had to be lifted out of the frames, for inspection and rebuilding.**

Bottom left: **The IMR had been looking for a diesel locomotive for many years – indeed I recall sitting in Sir Philip Wombwell's office back in 1967 as he tried to negotiate with CIE over the redundant diesel engines from the closed 3ft gauge West Clare section. A diesel engine finally arrived in July 1992, from Germany. It was a 200 hp Schoema diesel with a Deutz V12 engine and Voith hydraulic transmission. She was built by Christoph Schottler GmbH in 1958, and had previously worked at Helmstedt, north of Berlin. She weighs 26 tons and has a top speed of 33 km/h (ie just under 20 mph).**

Below: **The rebuild of the Gibbins Crane, and of No 8 *Fenella* were dreams my father and I both shared. He took a keen interest in both projects, but was not destined to see No 8 in steam. His contribution to the steam railway was a very considerable one, and as this portrait of the IOMR draws to a close, I think it fitting to show him with the IMR crane upon its arrival at Union Mills in May 1991. When new in 1893 it cost £267.0s.4d (£267.02).**

Chapter Two

HORSES, CABLES AND STEAM

IN DOUGLAS

In the early 1870's Douglas was rapidly developing as a seaside resort, and a retired Sheffield contractor, Thomas Lightfoot, who came to live in the town, proposed a horse tramway along the promenade then being built. An Act of Tynwald was obtained in 1876 and the first section, from Burnt Mill Hill to what is now the foot of Broadway, opened on 7th August 1876. It was extended to near the Victoria Pier early in 1877. In 1882, Lightfoot sold the tramway to a new concern, Isle of Man Tramways Ltd. In the 1880s more cars were added, and the line was doubled. Derby Castle, at the north of the as yet incomplete promenade, was a major entertainment centre, and the tramway was extended to Derby Castle gates in 1890. By 1891, there were 26 cars in use.

In 1893 the first section of the Electric Railway opened from Derby Castle to Groudle, and in May 1894, the horse tramway was acquired by the new Isle of Man Tramways & Electric Power Co, which envisaged electrifying the line, and working its cars right through to the Victoria Pier. Lengthy negotiations with Douglas Corporation ensued. In return for an extension of the 21-year compulsory purchase

period, after which the Corporation could take over the line, the IOMT&EPCo agreed to build a cable tramway to Upper Douglas. This would run from Victoria Pier, up Victoria Street, Buck's Road, and Woodbourne Road, and then via York Road, where the winding house and depot would be, back to the Promenade at Broadway. The line opened 15th August 1896.

Negotiations to electrify the horse tramway faltered, and in 1900 the IOMT&EPCo was dragged into ruin, following the collapse of Dumbell's Bank. The horse and cable tramways were purchased by Douglas Corporation in 1902. By now there were 36 horse cars and 12 cable cars. Electrification of both lines was discussed from time to time, but did not materialise.

In 1914, Douglas Corporation acquired its first motor buses, and the bus fleet expanded rapidly in the 1920s. The winter horse tram service succumbed to buses in 1927, and the cable cars, which had been seasonal since the winter of 1921-22, last ran on 19th August 1929. The horse cars became an 'institution', and three new cars arrived as late as 1935!

The service was suspended during the

Second World War, but resumed in 1946. Although the tramway survived, irresponsible agitation over alleged cruelty to horses resulted in the historic double deckers being broken up with one exception. The critics, seeing the large tram, immediately jump to ludicrous conclusions. They do not realise that the rolling resistance of a rail vehicle is around 10 lbs per ton, or less with roller bearings, whilst the resistance on Asphalt is about 43 lbs per ton, and on smooth grass land about 300 lbs per ton.

The horse tramway continues in operation, although the level of services has fallen as the number of visitors has declined. Douglas Corporation buses were merged into IOM National Transport in 1976.

Below: **With the destruction of the early double deckers, No's 1-8, the most historic cars were the first open toast-racks, 9 and 10, built by Starbuck in 1884. No 9 was broken up in the 1950s, but 10, depicted passing the Gaiety Theatre on 1st June 1963, survived until the late 1980s.**

Left: **A batch of second hand cars, numbered 13 to 18 arrived from South Shields in 1887. One double decker, No 14 (originally 13) survived the post war slaughter, and through the prompting of Keith Pearson was preserved, first at Clapham, and then returned to the IOM, under the ownership of the Science Museum. It ran in occasional service, and is seen here in May 1984. In the winter of 1990-91, a new gallery was opened at the Manx Museum, with No 14 being a centrepiece of the display.**

Centre: **As the Science Museum did not permit DCT to use the double decker, No 14, in regular service, the DCT manager, Wilson Gibb had the imaginative idea of returning single deck saloon No 18, to its original double decker condition. The newly rebuilt double decker is seen leaving Derby Castle on 29th May 1990 shortly after its return to service.**

Bottom left: **Two toast-racks came from Milnes in 1890, Nos 21 and 22. In 1908, 22 was rebuilt with a ridged roof. Two similar rebuilds were scrapped in the 'fifties, leaving 22 as the sole example. We see her in the car shed at Derby Castle in the 1970s, prior to reconstruction as the DCT 'tram shop'.**

Below: **York Road depot housed the DCT buses as well as the cable cars, and when the cable section closed down, the old boiler house became a repair bay. No 47, a Milnes Voss bulkhead from 1911 was one of the last cars to leave the depot in 1982, when she was preserved by the IOM Railway Society. The depot was later demolished and housing erected on the site.**

Right: **Cars 48 to 50 were built by Vulcan Motors in 1935, and were convertibles, with sliding shutters for bad weather. No 50 is seen with the shutters closed in August 1966. Having limited seating accommodation, they were never liked, and handed to IMR as station shelters in the late seventies. Nos 48 and 50 were broken up, but No 49 was rescued by the IOM Railway Society.**

Centre: **Maintenance work was centred on the cable car depot at York Road, with horse cars towed to and from York Road, behind a cable tram. When the cable section closed in 1929, horse trams were taken to York Road on a special trolley, towed behind a DCT bus! Car 32, a Milnes 'sunshade' toast-rack, is seen en route from Derby Castle to York Road in 1976. She was later rebuilt with bulkheads.**

Below: **IOM Passenger Transport applied an all over Advertising livery on some buses in the early 'eighties. DCT briefly followed suit with the results seen here on No 43, which had been built by the United Electric Car Co in 1907 as the first roofed toast-rack or 'bulkhead' car.**

Bottom: **A sister tram, 44, was used by the Queen Mother in 1963, and received end panels with the Corporation arms. She is heading for the Victoria Pier in May 1967.**

PRESERVED
DOUGLAS TRAMS

Top left: In the space of a few months in 1982, the Isle of Man Railway Society had to rescue no fewer than three horse cars, for with the imminent demolition of York Road depot, the Corporation had no space for the two cars which were lying there, Nos 11 and 47. In addition IOM Railways had found that the 48 to 50 series cars were not suitable for conversion to wayside shelters on the MER. The first car to move was DCT 49, which commenced its journey to the Ramsey railway museum, which was then run by the

Society, on board the DCT tram transporter. Whilst this was suitable for the short run from Derby Castle to York Road, the bearings overheated causing one of the tyres to catch fire! No 49 spent the night in the Glen Mona Hotel car park, and I have always wondered what the effect upon any late night reveller may have been, of discovering a Douglas horse tram at Glen Mona!

Top right: Both my parents had vivid memories of the cable cars running to Upper Douglas. In 1965 we heard that two cars had been 'discovered' in the north of the Island near Jurby, in use as a bungalow, and went to photograph them. They might have a chimney stack, but were still on their original bogies!

A few years later, Keith Pearson founded the Douglas Cable Car Group, and in an imaginative project, rescued the two cars in order to re-create a Douglas cable car.

Above: This is what Keith accomplished. It was a remarkable achievement, made all the more so, by the small size of the group. In dismantling the two cars, Keith discovered that they were No's 72 and 73, two of the original 1896 Milnes cross bench cars. As parts of both were used in the restored vehicle, it was numbered 72 at one end and 73 at the other. It has made occasional trips along Douglas Promenade, but in the absence of cable haulage, is propelled by a Land Rover. No 72/73 is at the Jubilee Clock in May 1985.

DCT BUSES

Right: Douglas Corporation began bus operations in 1914, and after acquiring Tilling Stevens petrol electrics for some years, standardised on AEC Regent double deckers from 1933, in a connection which was to last for 35 years! DCT 61~ seen at the Douglas Sea Terminal in July 1970, was a 1948 AEC Regent III. She was handed to National Transport in 1976, but was withdrawn the following year.

Below: DCT 31 was a very rare beast indeed, for she was an AEC Regal IV demonstrator. The Regal series had been the half-cab single deck version of the Regent, and the underfloor-engined Regal IV was a transition step to the later AEC Reliance. Built in 1950, she joined DCT a year later, but owing to a one-man operating agreement for smaller single deckers, was little used until 1970, when she was captured approaching Lord Street. She succumbed in the late 'seventies.

Below: **Five Guy Otter single deckers were acquired in 1957 to replace some of the pre-war Leyland Cubs which were the subject of the special one-man agreement. C F Wolsey, the DCT manager, felt that visitors would welcome comprehensive route information, and the buses, with their enormous humps became 'camels' to the DCT men. No 9 is in the quaint depot yard at York Road in September 1969.**

Bottom: **One of the routes operated by the Corporation served the steam railway station, and we can admire the classic lines of another Regent III, DCT 64, as a former Lancashire United Transport Leyland Tiger Cub, DCT 36, manoeuvers in the distance.**

Opposite top left: **With the spread of the rear engined double decker, production of the traditional front engined AEC Regent came to a close in 1968. DCT bought the very last Regent V to come off the production line. She became DCT 15, and is seen at Greensill's corner a year after she entered service. She was handed over to IOM National Transport, remaining in service until 1984**

Top right and bottom right: **To the visitor looking across Douglas Bay, the Falcon Cliff stands out as a fairy-tale Castle perched upon the cliff face overlooking the northern part of the promenade. The Falcon Cliff, was in fact an hotel and pub, and a cliff lift was built as early as 1887, but fell out of use, and was re-erected at Port Soderick. A new lift running on 5ft gauge metals, was built in 1927. It ran** until the start of the 1990s, but sale of the hotel, and plans to convert it to office use, mean that the fate of the Falcon Cliff lift hangs in the balance.

Bottom left: **The Isle of Man is associated with narrow gauge railways. Our last illustration was of a 5ft broad gauge system. We will now double the track gauge, to look at the IOM Harbour Board's** steam crane No 1 in action on 5th September 1969. No 1 spent most of her time within the confines of the oil terminal at the foot of the Battery Pier in Douglas, so was seldom photographed, and her trips along the sinuous 10ft gauge track on to the Battery Pier were infrequent. She fell victim to the greater flexibility of modern road cranes and alterations at the pier foot.

Chapter Three

THE MANX

ELECTRIC RAILWAY

The difficult terrain lying north of Douglas and the formidable 600 foot cliffs to the north of Laxey were key factors in the adoption of a west coast route when the steam railway was extended to Ramsey in 1879. The price was a 50% increase in mileage, but with steam traction, any alternative would have been costly to engineer and operate.

Even as the Manx Northern was being built, technology was taking a step forward, for Werner von Siemens displayed a diminutive electric locomotive at the Berlin Exhibition of 1879. It was little more than a novelty ride, but by 1881, a tramway was in operation in Berlin, and two lines followed in the British Isles in 1883, the short Volk's Electric Railway in Brighton and the much longer Giants Causeway Tramway in Ulster. In 1885, Blackpool introduced its first tramcars. With each new line, electric traction took another stride, yet even in the United States, where progress was fastest, as late as 1888, there were no more than a dozen

tramways with some 48 miles of track. The first electric section of the London Underground, the City & South London, followed in 1890, but it was not until 1893 that there was real progress.

On Merseyside, the Liverpool Overhead Railway was taking shape. It was the first elevated electric railway in the world, and had an enormous carrying capacity. In America, electric traction outgrew its humble streetcar beginnings with the opening of a 15 mile electric railway between Portland and Oregon City. A similar line opened later the same year, and a new term was coined, the inter-urban electric railroad. By 1917, nearly 10,000 cars rode more than 18,000 miles of intercity electric railroad in the United States alone. The other important event of 1893 was the completion of the first section of what was to become the Manx Electric Railway, the Island's own inter-urban electric railroad. A tiny community of 50,000 people in the middle of the Irish Sea was at the cutting edge of technology, and astonishing though

that was, what is even more miraculous is that whilst all the contemporary or earlier lines have either long gone or changed out of all recognition, the Manx Electric survived little altered from its inception in the 1890s to celebrate its centenary in the 1990s.

The story begins with a Scotsman, Alexander Bruce, manager of Dumbell's Bank. In 1889 Bruce joined forces with an engineer, Frederick Saunderson to develop the Howstrake estate, lying to the north of Douglas. This needed an Act of Tynwald, the Howstrake Estate Act of 1892. One clause provided for sewers, gas, electric and water mains. The same clause authorised a tramway to be worked by animal, steam, electric or other power. It was on this muted note that the Island moved to the forefront of technology. As construction of the first $2\frac{1}{4}$ miles, from Douglas to Groudle was under way, Bruce and his colleagues returned to Tynwald with proposals to take the line on to Laxey. The estate tramway was to become a fully fledged electric railway.

Facing page: **The estate tramway, for it could not yet be called an inter-urban railway, opened with three long bogie cars built by G F Milnes in 1893. They were re-equipped with new power trucks in 1903, and one was lost in a depot fire in 1930, but the other two cars survived due to the inability of the MER to modernise its system from the 1920s onwards. No 1 poses outside No 1 Car shed at Derby Castle depot, with the author at the controls, on 31st August 1963.**

Right: **It was hoped that the cars would be able to haul two trailers, so six open toast-racks were also acquired. They received a lightweight roof in 1894, and became known as 'Umbrella cars'. Five were later rebuilt with wooden bulkhead ends. A sixth car, No 52, was left as an umbrella, losing her roof and seats each winter for PW duties. By the 1950s, she was no longer needed in passenger use, but the roof lay in store in Derby Castle depot. In the early 'eighties, it dawned on my father and I that all the bits to re-create an umbrella car existed. The MER engineers were not prepared to relinquish their PW flat, but suggested that as the roof on No 51 was in poor condition, she should receive the Umbrella roof. The trailers were originally numbered 11 to 16, being renumbered to make way for later power cars, and the rebuild became No 13. She is depicted in Derby Castle yard with the dash part lettered in May 1987.**

Centre: **The ground rose steeply to the north of Derby Castle, and an immense embankment carried the line up the side of the cliffs at 1 in 24. No 6, carrying an ornate 'Isle of Man Passenger Transport' insignia heads down grade into Douglas past the now demolished Douglas Bay Hotel.**

Below: **The line commenced from an end on junction with the Douglas horse trams at Derby Castle. No 9, one of the 1894 power cars, is manoeuvring prior to taking a party of visiting American traction fans on 4th July 1977. At that time, the elegant shelter still spanned the horse tram tracks.**

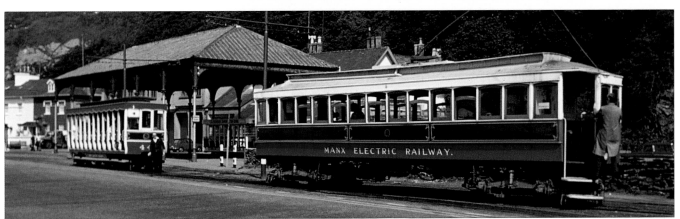

Top: **The tramway was paralleled by a toll road. Despite modern ribbon development, open country is reached within 1¼ miles at Far End. No 2, the other surviving 1893 car, was restored to original livery prior to this 1981 study.**

Centre: **A holiday camp, now closed, developed at Howstrake, and an arched waiting shelter was built. Car 20 squeals round the curve en route for Douglas on a summer's evening in 1990.**

Below: **Beyond Howstrake, the line turned inland, and dropped sharply as far as Groudle, 2¼ miles from Douglas. The Groudle river had cut a picturesque valley, and Groudle Glen became the terminus when the line opened on 7th September 1893. Services ceased at the end of the month, and work began on the Laxey extension. One of the seldom used 1898 'ECC' toast-racks, so named, after their power trucks, built by the Electric Construction Co of Wolverhampton, pauses at Groudle with trailer 60 in 1983.**

Right: **As far as the Lancashire Arms, where the line met the Douglas-Laxey road, it kept to its private right of way with its toll road alongside, but north of Baldromma, the line followed the main road for some distance, but was separated from it by walling. No 9, one of six enclosed saloons built for the opening of the Laxey section in 1894, is on PW (permanent way) duties near Scarffe's Crossing in March 1982. She has been restored to late 1890s livery.**

Below: **The 1894 cars, with their long narrow bodies, and longitudinal seating, received the nickname 'tunnel cars'. This 1963 portrait of a passengers view of No 9 shows her little altered from the day she arrived!**

Bottom: **The line opened to Laxey on 28th July 1894, to a terminus south of Rencell Lane, near the present car sheds. In the winter of 1895-96 it was extended over the lane to a new terminus. No 9 heads trailer 47 towards Rencell Lane bridge past the site of the 1896 terminus on a sunny 2nd September 1975.**

LAXEY

Left: **The present Laxey station enjoyed a strangely nebulous status, for it was neither a part of the original Douglas-Laxey line, nor of the Ramsey line proper, but a kind of appendage linking the two. Operationally it fits with the Douglas section, so is best considered now. The ground dropped away sharply beyond the 1896 terminus, and the line was carried across the valley on a graceful battlemented viaduct. Car 25 heads into Laxey station in 1975.**

Bottom left: **Laxey station was laid out in a pleasant wooded site in the grounds of Christ Church and the mine captain's house. Small rustic kiosks appeared as in this classic 1961 scene at Laxey. The white building in the distance, now the Mines Tavern, was formerly the mine captain's house, the south wing of which had to be demolished to make way for the railway lines. The station building is to the right, and typifies the 'rustic' style adopted by the IOMT&EPCo, with branches nailed to a wooden structure.**

Below: **Nowadays we take electric power for granted but the MER, in the 1890s, had to build its own power stations as well as its railway. By 1903 the original 550V dc transmission system was archaic, so rapid had been progress, and a 7kV ac HT feeder system was added. In 1935 the MER gave up power generation, taking power from the IOM Electricity Board instead. A new sub station was built near the site of the 1894 station, to become the hub of the power distribution system, taking power at 33kV, and transforming it to 575V DC for 550V line use, or 6.6kV for transmission via feeders to other sub-stations. The old marble switch panels on the dc side were re-used.**

ONWARDS TO SNAEFELL

Top: **In January 1895, Bruce and his colleagues formed the Snaefell Mountain Railway Association to build a mountain railway from Laxey to the summit of Snaefell. SMR No 4 enters the 1898 joint station in August 1960. She was one of a handful of cars to receive the MER Board 1957 green and white livery, and the last to carry it, in September 1963.**

Centre: **The joint station was in fact the third SMR terminus, its immediate predecessor being by the junction of the Laxey to Ramsey highway and the road up to the lead mines. Car 1 appears to be descending, but as right hand running is practised on the SMR, is in fact beginning the climb. The houses to the left, officially Dumbell's Row, were known as 'Ham and Egg Terrace', for they were occupied by miners, whose wives supplemented family income by providing ham and egg teas for the visitors.**

Bottom right: **As MER 21 heads north with a Ramsey working, SMR 6 drops down the hill towards Laxey. The roof of the Laxey station goods shed can be seen beyond and to the right of SMR 6, whilst an MER car and trailer sit in the siding next to the goods depot.**

Below: **The electric railway adopted the 'Three Legs of Mann' as its heraldic device. For most of the railway's existence it has appeared on the varnished wood panels or against the red background of those cars with steel dash panels. I have chosen to illustrate it on one of the green cars in the short-lived and controversial MER Board 1957 livery.**

Top: **When the Snaefell line was built in 1895, it did not drop down to road level, but ran along the valley side to a combined station and car shed. In 1897, the line was extended to the temporary road side terminus. This necessitated a point on the 1 in 12 gradient, which posed a serious problem, for due to the severe grade, the line was built on the Fell system with a centre rail for braking. This could not be interrupted for obvious reasons. Instead of an ordinary point, it was necessary to move running rails and brake rail by a series of cranks from the main line to the depot road! Car 1 passes the depot point in 1971. This amazing point survived until the cars were fitted with new motors and rheostatic braking, when an ordinary point was substituted.**

Below left: **Calliper brake shoes gripped the running rail, and as this was a friction brake, sliding on a rough rail for virtually the whole journey, wear on the brake shoes was so heavy that they often lasted for no more than three trips. Stanley Cannell changes the shoes on car No 3 in September 1969.**

Below, centre: **The cars were 'state of the art' in 1895, and retained their original equipment until the late 1970s, as in this portrait of car No 2. Whilst the coastline had been built to the usual Manx 3ft gauge, the Snaefell section was to 3ft 6in. It is often said that this was to house the Fell brake equipment, but the real reason was more fundamental. Bruce and his colleagues believed that with four 25hp**

motors, the cars could tackle the 1 in 12 grade, which was twice as steep as the coastline, but they could not be sure. However the Fell system could be used for additional traction as well as braking, and by allowing the wider gauge, it would be possible to add an extra motor to each truck to drive on the centre rail if need be. As it happened, the cars managed, but it was a wise precaution.

Below right: **The light weight coast bogies are moved about by hand, but the heavy SMR trucks, with their motors are either towed by another Snaefell car, or moved by pinch bar.**

THE CLIMB TO SNAEFELL

Above: **When one considers that electric traction was then in its infancy, it is amazing that the 1895 motors were able to operate successfully until the 1970s, but they were becoming increasingly unreliable, and a search began for replacement motors. Some 1950s built motors came from the closed Aachen tramway in Germany, and the first SMR car to be rebuilt was No 1, in 1977. The rest of the fleet followed in 1978-79. The rebuilds were distinguished by their enhanced performance, and also the roof mounted rheostatic braking system. SMR 2 is on the isolated Lhergy Veg section, remote from roads, and where the line briefly levels out, and even drops slightly, before resuming the 1 in 12 climb.**

Centre: **SMR 6, in rebuilt guise, tackles the Lhergy Veg section en route to the summit. Owing to the steepness of the valley, retaining walls were necessary on parts of this section.**

Right: **With 1895 technology, four miles was an impossible distance to transmit power, and a mid-position location was selected for the power house, where the valley flank opened out a little below the crossing with the mountain road. By 1903-04 dc transmission of power was archaic, and a new 7kV ac system was grafted on to the existing coast and mountain lines. The SMR power house remained in use at peak periods until 1924, but since that date has functioned as a sub-station only. No 6 passes the power house in May 1989.**

Top left: **The SMR crossed the Douglas-Ramsey mountain road at 'the Bungalow', so named after a large hotel which was built there. Rather than show the familiar 'Bungalow' scene, I have selected a portrait of car No 1 towing rail bogies, crossing the road in February 1976.**

Top right: **Car 3, with original equipment and roof boards, drops down near the North Shoulder in September 1969, with one of the peaks of North Barrule, the second highest spot in Mann, visible in the distance. Owing to high winds, the overhead is taken down on the final section to the summit each winter. The Snaefell Mountain Railway Association had only been formed in January 1895, yet so rapid was progress that the line was opened on 21st August 1895.**

Above: **At the summit, a large wooden hotel was constructed. This was replaced in 1906 by a battlemented masonry structure. This lost much of its decoration in post-war refurbishment, but survived little altered until a disastrous fire in the 1980s, after which it was rebuilt. We see SMR No 2 by the hotel in August 1965.**

Above: **Maintenance facilities at the SMR depot at Laxey were rudimentary, and with the 6in difference in gauge, SMR cars could not work through. In 1932 the railway came up with the answer; a mixed gauge siding was laid in at Laxey, and SMR cars were jacked up, fitted with 3ft gauge spare trailer trucks and could then be towed in and out of Douglas. SMR 2 heads past Laxey MER car shed at the site of the 1894 station en route to the mixed gauge siding in May 1975.**

Centre: **As car 20 heads southbound on a service working, SMR 2 is propelled over the connection from the 3ft coast line to the dual gauge section.**

Left: **The SMR car is positioned on the mixed gauge track, and then one end is jacked up. The short 3ft gauge bogie is run out and the body is then traversed some three inches to centre it for the Mountain bogie, as it is triple rather than quadruple rail mixed gauge. The car is then lowered onto the longer (and higher) SMR bogie. The process will be repeated at the other end.**

Left: On 16th August 1970, only a few days prior to the 75th birthday of the Snaefell section, No 5 caught fire at the summit, and a strong wind fanned the blaze with the freakish result that although most of the body was totally destroyed, the breeze kept the flames away from the lower end bulkhead, and the paint on the number panel was not even scorched!

Centre: The MER rose to the challenge, and whilst railway staff refurbished the chassis and electrical equipment, a new body was fabricated by H D Kinnin, Joinery manufacturers of Ramsey. The rebuild is seen outside the SMR depot on 22nd June 1971, just before completion.

Below right: In 1950, the Air Ministry established a radar station on the summit of Snaefell. This meant the overhead had to be left in situ, with consequent risk of damage. The following year, the Air Ministry supplied a small four wheeled Wickham railcar with a Ford V8 petrol engine. A small shed was built at Laxey to house the railcar. Initially painted in RAF blue, it is seen in the later CAA colours at the bungalow in May 1975.

Bottom right: In 1957, a larger Wickham car, with a goods portion was delivered. This also carried 'Air Force Blue' for some years, but was later painted in a high visibility yellow and black paint scheme.

Bottom left: By 1977, when a third railcar arrived, the Civil Aviation Authority had taken over, and the new Wickham car, which is fitted with a Perkins 4.208 diesel, is seen with the 1957 car in the background. The original 1951 car was sold to the SMR for departmental use. A fourth car arrived in 1992, permitting disposal of the 1957 unit.

A 'ROYAL' TRAM

Top: 1895 was an important year for Alexander Bruce and his colleagues, for apart from completing the Snaefell line, they took delivery of a short 4-wheel directors saloon. As this rode very badly, it was mounted on bogies in 1900, and was used by King Edward VII and Queen Alexandra in August 1902. Before the war, coast line cars had carried a similar livery to the Snaefell section, with the red panel edged in white, but this was dropped as an economy measure, and the only car to retain it, until the old style was re-introduced in 1979, was the Royal trailer No 59.

Above, left: No 59 also retained its original red velvet upholstery and ornate internal fittings. There is disagreement as to which seat was occupied by King Edward VII, and at different times, old hands have pointed out three different seats as 'the' royal seat! No 59 is occasionally used in traffic, but as befits its royal status and historic upholstery, its use is limited.

Above, right: In 1896 only one vehicle was added to the fleet, trailer No 60, which is seen here in the 'varnished post' livery, heading past Laxey car shed on 28th August 1963. The late Roy Cannell, who was chief engineer for many years, was always puzzled by various bolt holes, obviously unused since the trailer was delivered. When Roy was helping Keith Pearson with the rebuild of the Douglas cable car, he found that chassis had similar bolt holes, and concluded that 60, which has identical seat end grab rails to the cable cars, was in effect a cable car chassis diverted to the MER!

NORTH OF LAXEY

Above: **Work began on the Laxey-Ramsey section in 1898. Just beyond Laxey station, the line crossed over the washing floors of the Mines, making a U turn, and climbed up the north side of the Laxey valley. No 9 approaches the level crossing over the Ramsey road in 1981. This was one of four cars repainted in historic liveries for the 1979 Millennium of Tynwald celebrations and the centenary of Electric traction (celebrating the original Siemens line in Berlin).**

Centre: **The line climbs almost continuously at 1 in 27/28/24 to a summit at Ballaragh, 588ft above sea level. The highlight is the 500ft-plus cliffside shelf at Bulgham. As Colin Goldsmith, works supervisor at the steam railway, but on the Electric for the day, looks on, toast-rack No 25 negotiates the crossover at Ballaragh with the weed-killer wagon in 1990.**

Left: **The weed-killer is mounted on an old 4-wheel wagon, and as soon as it is on the 'seaside' track, Colin sets to work. The tank, which was shared with the steam railway after the systems merged, is about life expired and is to be replaced in 1993.**

Right: The Ballaragh section with a 500ft drop to the sea, and cliffs climbing 70ft above rail level, must be one of the most spectacular railway vantage points in the British Isles, as this portrait of No 20 testifies. Construction was extremely difficult, and necessitated a partially cantilevered formation at one point.

Centre: On 20th January 1967, a part of the formation collapsed, and whilst remedial work went on, cars terminated each side of the breach. As work could not be completed before the start of summer services, additional cars were gingerly edged over the landside track, including No 6, which is seen with trailer 44 at the north side of the breach on 31st May 1967. Through running resumed on 10th July.

Below: In July 1977 a party of American railfans from the Electric Railroaders Association visited the Island. My father and I had arranged a slide evening for MER staff, and the US party were invited to join us. Afterwards they invited us to join them on their 'special' the following day, to help with photo stops. The most celebrated American narrow gauge railroad is the Silverton branch of the Rio Grande, and one of their party turned to us at Ballaragh, and said 'this is an electric Silverton', which was a big compliment! The ERA special, Nos 9, 44 and van 11 is seen at Ballaragh on 4th July 1977.

Above: **Tommy Senogles is at the controls of green car No 27 at Dhoon Glen station, a few hundred yards north of Ballaragh in August 1960. No 27 was one of a handful of toast-racks which received the green paint scheme. The differing level of the stepboards is to clear the Brush trucks which these cars are fitted with, and led to their being nicknamed 'paddleboxes'.**

Centre: **North of Laxey, the line deserts the highway for much of the journey into Ramsey, and it is along this section that some of the most striking scenic locations are to be found. No 5 and trailer No 45 head south on the 6.30pm ex Ramsey at Ballafayle on 25th August 1972.**

Left: **The approach to Ramsey is dramatic, with views of Ramsey Bay and the Queens Pier opening out. Nos 20 and 40 are heading south through Belle Vue on the 8th September 1963. Four big saloons were delivered in 1899, No's 19 to 22. They received trucks which had been delivered the previous year, but such had been the progress in electric equipment, that they exchanged trucks with four newly delivered toast-racks (28 to 31) in 1904, to give them improved performance, and have dominated the scheduled services ever since.**

Below: **As at Laxey, entry into the centre of Ramsey was blocked by a deep ravine, and the line opened to a temporary terminus at Ballure on 2nd August 1898. During the winter of 1898-99, an imposing two span lattice viaduct was erected by Francis Morton & Co of Liverpool. Winter Saloon**

No 19, restored to 1930s MERCo livery, heads south across the viaduct in March 1982.

Below right: **It is sometimes claimed that relaying or repainting is a sure sign of imminent closure, and the relaying of the** level crossing just north of Ballure viaduct in February 1974 was indeed ominous, for political support was at its lowest ebb, and the Laxey to Ramsey section was to close on 30th September 1975.

Bottom right: **When permanent way repairs are called for, single line working is instituted, using conventional train staffs, the section being adjusted according to circumstances. The 'Ramsey' inscription merely indicates that this staff is kept at Ramsey station, for use on the northern part of the route.**

Below: **Overhead repairs also necessitate single line working, and specialised skills. A new length of trolley wire is being rigged on the Ramsey section in this scene. John Duggan, on the right, with a father and many other relations on the line, typifies the family traditions behind the Manx Electric.**

RAMSEY

Above: **In 1904, the MER acquired two saloon trailers, Nos 57 and 58. They were luxurious vehicles and were fitted with air brakes. As trailers were seldom needed in winter, and in summer, most passengers preferred the open trailers, they have seen little use. The first time my father photographed 58 in service was on 12th April 1963, when she came into Ramsey.**

Centre: **A seashore approach to Ramsey was discussed, but the final route was inland to a terminus by the Palace music hall, later the Plaza cinema, recently demolished. For a time this was owned by the railway. Shunting was complex, especially if a goods van was in use. Car 22 has moved to the Douglas side of the train. Van 12 has been shunted to the seaside track for the return journey, but trailer 41 is still on the landside track.**

Left: **In its heyday, the MER operated early morning boat specials, late evening services and even mail runs, for it functioned in the same way as the American inter-urbans. Evening services still run in July and August, but the days when the last car from Ramsey was as late as 10.30pm are long gone. In fact, No 19 is seen on the last 10.30 service, on 26th August 1972.**

In view of our family association with the Isle of Man, I always felt that my parents showed a lack of foresight in not being on the Island when I arrived, though I should have considered the matter too! It was agreed that my 21st birthday *would* be on the Island. We arrived the day before, and when we woke up the next morning, it was to discover a carpet of snow and a glorious blue sky. A fair part of the day was spent chasing electric cars, including appropriately, No 21 at Dhoon Plat.

This view from 7th February 1969 combines two of the Island's transport systems, MER car 21, and in the background the Laxey depot of Isle of Man Road Services, with a double decker visible inside the garage. No 21 still graces MER metals, but the bus and the Laxey depot are now no more. There is much to be said just for having a birthday in February if it offers this sort of photographic chance. Any reader unsure of which month he would like to be born in, might take note!

Top: When Alexander Bruce and his colleagues started their revolutionary new scheme in 1893, they were hesitant as to accepting freight traffic, but by 1894 they were less nervous, and with Tynwald imposing the duty to carry mails, merchandise and parcels, they felt they had better equip themselves. By the turn of the century, a dozen 4-wheel wagons had arrived, some of which we have already seen. Goods sheds had appeared at Douglas, Laxey and Ramsey. No 19 passes the Laxey goods depot with trailer 45 and van 11.

Above left: At Ballaragh, we encountered one of the open wagons minus sides in use on weed-killing duties. Car 29, in the charge of Johnny Corkill and Bertie Dawson crosses Mines Road, Laxey with wagon 7 on 9th September 1963. No 29 was one of the four toast-racks built in 1904 which surrendered its trucks to the winter saloons, Nos 19 to 22, receiving the 1898 equipment in lieu .

Above right: In 1895, four utility passenger cars had been built, and were numbered 10 to 13. They had glazed compartments for the drivers, but the passenger section was unglazed. They were not popular, and

were put into store in 1902. One later became a motor freight car, a second became a motor cattle car, and two became freight trailers. No 10 became freight trailer 26, and in our first book on the MER, published in 1978, my father and I wrote 'No 26 would make an invaluable museum exhibit'. There is nothing better than being able to quote the authority of a book, even if you wrote it. This view was taken on 31st May 1979 when freight car 26, by then owned by the IOM Railway Society, was en route to the new Railway Museum at Ramsey! The Museum was operated very successfully by the society for over a decade.

Below: Apart from 4-wheel opens, the MER also built a number of bogie opens, one of which survived to receive a pair of Challenger 1600 PW cranes in 1977. She is seen at the Dhoon sidings fresh from the shops on PW duty. The Dhoon is an appropriate location, for two quarries, one connected by skip wagons, the other one by an aerial ropeway, contributed stone traffic to the railway.

Centre left: A second quarry existed at Dreemsherry, and the head-shunt, siding up to the tipping dock and narrow gauge quarry lines were still intact, if overgrown in the early 'seventies.

Centre right: The tipping dock at Dreemskerry. The 'two foot' lines on the trestle ran into the now overgrown quarry, and manually propelled tip wagons were used to load the MER open wagons on the 'three foot' siding.

Bottom: The MER provided collection and delivery facilities at Douglas and Ramsey. The Ramsey van looked more at home in the 1957 green and white livery than the power cars did. The illustration on the side of the Austin van was hand painted.

Some customers collected or delivered their own goods at Ramsey, and the driver of the Clucas' steam laundry van has backed his Bedford as close to MER goods van 14 as possible!

The MER conveyed mail between Douglas and Ramsey until all year services ended in 1975. Mail is being transferred between MER van 11 and a GPO Morris van in June 1971.

With large quantities of stone moving over the system, the IOMT&EPCo felt they needed an electric locomotive, and No 23 emerged from Derby Castle depot in 1900. As built, she was a centre cab engine with sloping bonnets at each end, and borrowed power trucks from a passenger car in winter when freight traffic was at its heaviest. She was involved in an accident in 1914, and lay in store until 1925-26 when she emerged on a lengthened frame. Instead of sloping bonnets to house weights, the MER provided 6 ton wagon bodies, reasoning that when conveying stone the wagon bodies too would be laden, giving adhesion, and when returning light, they would also be empty, reducing the need for adhesion! In 1978 we wrote 'it would be pleasant to see it restored and on display'. A year later, under the ownership of the IOM Railway Society, she was! In 1983 and 1984 she made a limited number of trips, borrowing power trucks once more, and is expected to run again during the 1993 Centenary celebrations.

FROM COMPANY
TO BOARD

At the close of 1899, the Isle of Man Tramways & Electric Power Co had written a brilliant chapter in engineering history. Within a few weeks, all was to change. On 3rd February 1900, Dumbell's Bank collapsed, due to massive loans to the electric railway and in support of other projects. The IOMT&EPCo, which had been so intimately associated with the bank, through Bruce, followed it into liquidation. A mainland syndicate put in the best bid for the line in 1902, and the line was sold to the newly formed Manx Electric Railway Co Ltd. The progress in electric traction since 1893 prompted the new owners to modernise the power supply system, and add new stock, the first deliveries being the four toast-rack cars, Nos 28 to 31, in 1904. The new cars soon lost their trucks to the winter cars, and in modern times have been little used. Car 31 basks in the sun at Derby Castle depot on 8th June 1963.

From 1903 to 1906 money flowed into the MER from its new owners, as the line was brought up to modern standards. This included not only the four 1904 cars, but replacement trucks for many of the older vehicles and two new toast-rack power cars in 1906. Nos 32 and 33 came from United Electric Car Co at Preston, and the latter climbs out of Laxey en route to Douglas with trailer 61 on 22nd June 1971. The new owners now settled back to enjoy the fruits of their investments, but the 1914-18 war intervened, and with arrears of debenture interest to make up, the MER was in no position to continue to modernise.

In the 'twenties, the Island suffered from the Depression, and the MER was struck with the misfortune of fire and flood in 1930, eating into reserves. The line soldiered on until the Second World War, when traffic was again affected. By the early 'fifties, the company was in dire straits, but showed itself more dedicated to the public interest than most politicians. Finally, through the efforts of Deemster Sir Percy Cowley, and of Sir Charles Kerruish, and the willingness of the MER to take less than scrap price, the line came into public ownership in 1957. Car 22, at Derby Castle in April 1959 carries the 'modern' green and white livery adopted by the new government-run MER Board.

Top: **The MER enjoyed a period of political support lasting roughly ten years, from 1957 to 1967 followed by a period in the wilderness, culminating in the closure of the Laxey-Ramsey section on 30th September 1975. This was based on the premise that no more than 25% of the traffic would be lost. My father suggested it would be nearer 50%. It was!**
A new House of Keys, elected in 1976 was more favourable to the MER, and the line re-opened on 25th June 1977, with the traditional tape cutting. Sir Charles Kerruish, Speaker of the House of Keys is to the left, Harold Gilmore, manager of the MER in the centre, and J J Christian, chairman of the MER Board to the right.

Above left: The inaugural Car, No 20, with trailer 57, has arrived at Ramsey station, both car and station being decorated for this happy occasion. It was thrilling to see the Ramsey section back in business after so many months of uncertainty.

Above right: 1977 was also the Silver Jubilee, and car 25 was specially turned out in silver livery to commemorate the occasion. Its usual trailer 55, was similarly bedecked, and temporarily renumbered 25. The Silver Jubilee set sits outside Laxey goods shed in June 1977.

TRIUMPH AND TRAGEDY

Right: **In 1978, Bill Jackson invited my father to represent IOM Railways on the Centenary of Electric Railways Committee. Within a few weeks, he had designed the CER logo, and persuaded the committee to make the IOM the centre piece of the UK celebrations! As 1979 was the Millennium of Tynwald this fitted in perfectly, and events included a cavalcade at Laxey, and the opening of a railway museum at Ramsey. I had suggested to Bill Jackson that a green toast-rack would complete the historic liveries, and the newly restored 32 came up to Ramsey a few days before the museum opened with the crane wagon to unload some exhibits.**

Centre: **In a charming gesture, as most of the exhibits were to be provided by the IOM Railway Society, Bill Jackson and John Christian invited Mrs Elaine Hendry to open the Museum on behalf of the Society. She felt John Christian should open it as Chairman of the MER Board. With them nominating one another, Bill Jackson said they had better both open it, which is how it happened!**

Below: **In September 1990, car 22 was burnt out due to an electrical fault, and a rebuild commenced much along the lines of the 1971 rebuild of SMR 5, with woodwork contracted to a Port Erin firm, McArds. The frame work is taking shape in Derby Castle depot in June 1991.**

Below right: **By September 1991, the reconstruction was sufficiently far advanced to transfer 22 from the main car shed to the paint shop. It was her first appearance in daylight since rebuilding began, and I have selected this scene in preference to the completed car, in order to show the complex framework of the Manx Electric stock.**

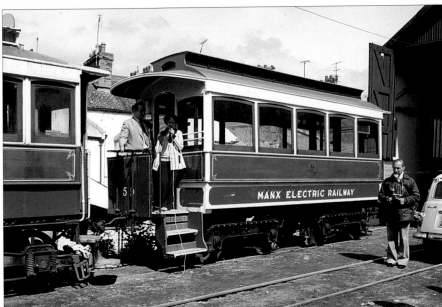

Left and below: **On 18th October 1991,** Dr R Preston Hendry passed away after a short illness. His association with the railways of the Island stretched back to 1917, and for over forty years. he had recorded them on film. For the last twenty five years, he had campaigned vigorously for their preservation, and the committee of the Isle of Man Railway Society decided that it would be a fitting tribute if MER loco No 23, which is the only locomotive ever built on the Island, and the oldest Bo-Bo electric engine in the British Isles, were named in his memory. Sir Charles Kerruish, President of Tynwald, in performing the unveiling ceremony on 25th May 1992, said of Dr Hendry, 'it is perhaps natural, that given his interest in transport systems generally, he became, as it were, an independent assessor of developments in the Isle of Man. A doughty fighter, he challenged forthrightly, governments and commercial interests alike, portraying the spirit and desire of those less eloquent in debate than himself, and portrayed it so meaningfully that it may well be claimed that it was his participation that was the factor that led to the continuation of the railway systems we have in operation in our Island today.' It was in fact a team effort; the railways had outstanding officers, A M Sheard, Donald Shaw and Roy Cannell to name but three. They had a dedicated and marvellous staff, and when even that combination was not enough, just enough people inside and outside government who fought for them, and overcame those of lesser vision.

Right: **As a tribute to the engineers, without whose skills, the line could not survive, we will visit Derby Castle depot. Until recent changes the paint shop comprised two tracks at the bottom of No 2 car shed. No 21 receives a repaint on 1st March 1977.**

Centre: **The main stabling area comprises Nos 2, 4 and 3 car sheds, though as all three are joined, the distinction is academic. We are looking up No 3 car shed on 31st August 1963. Road by road, the stock comprises 31, 14, 15 and 17, 44, 54, and 49, 55, 25, 56, 26, and trailer 62.**

Bottom: **In 1976-77 the MER began to rebuild the Snaefell cars with equipment from Aachen in Germany. Most of the Aachen cars went to London Transport, but one came to the Island, where it is seen in September 1977: the only modern tram to appear on the MER.**

STEAM ON THE MER

IMR and MNR engines had been hired during construction of the MER to haul materials. As part of the centenary events, steam trips were planned, and a trial run took place in December 1991. IMR No 4 Loch was transferred to the MER to run between Laxey and Dhoon Quarry Sidings. I attended the trials, but in the aftermath of my father's death, the views I took were misplaced, and Chris Milner of Railway Magazine kindly helped out. The evening Chris offered to help, my own views turned up, so I have included one of my own and two of Chris'.

Top: **Prior to the actual runs to the Dhoon on 5th December, *Loch* made a couple of run pasts in Laxey station flanked by MER and SMR cars.** Chris Milner.

Above left: **Chris caught *Loch* bringing the two MER saloon trailers Nos 57 and 58 into Laxey station prior to the various trips.** Chris Milner.

Above right: ***Loch* blasts up hill from Dhoon station towards the 588ft Ballaragh summit. The trials revealed that the engine had just sufficient power to handle the two-coach trains on the 1 in 24 grades out of Laxey.** Robert Hendry.

GROUDLE GLEN

AND OTHER LINES

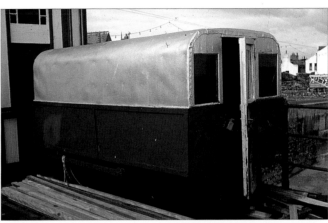

OTHER LINES

Apart from the main rail systems, the Island has a rich tapestry of other rail sites, three of which adjoined the Manx Electric.

Top left: **The oldest of these was the Laxey Mines Railway, which operated until the lead mines closed down during the Depression in 1929-30. The surface plant,**

including two small steam engines, vanished for scrap long ago, but some of the underground equipment was rescued by dedicated mines enthusiasts, and one of their early discoveries, a 4-wheel mine wagon is seen in August 1975.

Top right: **In July 1886, the 2,300 foot long Queen's Pier was opened to provide deep water facilities for passenger sailings to and from Ramsey. A 3ft gauge tramway was installed with small 4-wheel luggage trolleys. In 1899 a diminutive 4-wheel**

passenger car arrived. This was pushed by hand along the pier, and is the only manually propelled passenger vehicle the author has ever seen!

Above: **In May 1937, the IOM Harbour Board acquired a Hibberd 'Planet' petrol locomotive and bogie trailer, the wheels on the latter being not much larger than those on the average shopping trolley! The combination is seen on 27th August 1959. In July 1963, the Queen Mother travelled on the Pier Tramway.**

Top: **In 1950, the Harbour Board acquired an 11 seat Wickham petrol railcar driven by a Ford petrol engine. Its noise and vibration had to be experienced to be believed. In August 1959, it was painted cream with a red trim.**

Above left: **By 1972, it had become red with a silver trim, but the main reason for including this scene is that the pier tramway extended a short distance into the roadway, and this was the only occasion we ever photographed the tram on the road. The railcar went to IOM Railways but was later cut up.**

Above right: **In the 'eighties the Harbour Board closed the tramway, and the Planet loco and trailer were presented to the IOM Railway Society. They have made periodic trips along the MER from Ramsey station in conjunction with transport weekends organised by the society. Just prior to withdrawal from service, the Planet was re-engined and a new circular bonnet casing was fitted.**

I hope you have enjoyed this portrait of the railways of the Island, some still with us, others no more. Both the IOM Railway Society and Groudle Glen/IOM Supporters Association would welcome your help in their many projects.

The IOM Railway Society can be contacted c/o the author at:

4 Clifton Road
Rugby, Warwickshire
CV21 3PZ

They would welcome your support.

GROUDLE GLEN

The opening of the first section of the electric railway to Groudle in 1893 placed the glen on the tourist map, and an ambitious development plan ensued, with rustic paths leading to various attractions. Work began on a diminutive two foot gauge glen railway in 1895. The line opened in 1896 with a single Bagnall 2-4-0T. As a sea lion enclosure existed at the seaward end of the line, the engine was named accordingly. In 1906 a second Bagnall

2-4-0T came, this time named Polar Bear. The real Polar bears were a victim of the First World War, and the sea lions of the Second World War, by which time the outer cliffside section of the line was suffering from erosion, and was cut back to a loop on the headland.

Below left: **Services resumed that summer, and a visit in August 1961 to the Lhen Coan terminus with its delightful Swiss Chalet shelter revealed the coaches in a harlequin red and yellow livery.**

Below right: **The line closed in the late**

'fifties, but in April 1961 when we visited it, we found the coaches freshly undercoated outside the combined loco and coach shed at Lhen Coan terminus.

Bottom: *Polar Bear* was carrying an ornate red and blue livery with polished boiler bands. The other locomotive *Sea Lion,* lay derelict, pushed out of the back of the engine shed at Lhen Coan. *Polar Bear* went to Brockham, and later Amberley. She completed a major rebuild, and is expected to make a guest appearance at Groudle during 1993.

Left: Trains terminated at the headland loop, and on a summer's day, with the blue sea, vivid paint scheme, the gorse and the bracken, it was idyllic. Sadly it was a brief renaissance, and after two seasons, the line closed down again. The engines were sold, vandals tipped most of the carriages down the side of the glen, and in the 'seventies, the track was lifted.

Below: If it had not been for the Isle of Man Railway Supporters Association, the Groudle story would have ended on this sad note. In the early 'eighties, they began to re-create the Glen railway. Gorse and bracken was hacked away, drainage was restored, parts of the formation which had subsided were rebuilt, and two Hudson-Hunslet 4-wheel industrial diesels were acquired. GGR No 2 departs from the Lhen Coan in May 1985.

Top: **By May 1986, a roofed carriage had appeared, and *Dolphin* trundled through the wooded reaches of the upper glen.**

Above: ***Sea Lion*, disused since 1939, was rebuilt as part of an apprentice training scheme, by British Nuclear Fuels at Sellafield, and returned to the Glen, where it is here caught in a sylvan setting near the Lime Kiln crossing.**

Left: *Sea Lion* passes the ruins of the headland cafe during the summer of 1988.

Below: An even more ambitious project now began, as the ground was cut back to permit restoration of the outer section of the line from the Headland loop to the Sea Lion Rocks. By May 1991, track laying was in progress, and when a party of enthusiasts, led by my father, visited the Glen, *Sea Lion* was specially run out on to the first part of the extension for photographs. This was the view he took that day, and I can think of no more fitting view to conclude this portrait of 'Rails in the Isle of Man'. The extension opened in 1992.

Further information about Groudle Glen is available from:

Tony Beard
19 Ballabrooie Grove
Douglas
IOM.